Practical copyright for library and information professionals

Paul Pedley

facet publishing

© Paul Pedley 2015
Published by Facet Publishing
7 Ridgmount Street, London WC1E 7AE
www.facetpublishing.co.uk

Facet Publishing is wholly owned by CILIP: the Chartered Institute of
Library and Information Professionals.

Every purchase of a Facet book helps to fund CILIP's
advocacy, awareness and accreditation programmes
for information professionals.

British Library Cataloguing in Publication Data
A catalogue record for this book is available from the British Library.

ISBN 978-1-78330-061-7

First published 2015

Text printed on FSC accredited material.

Typeset from author's files in 10/13 pt Aldine 401 and Humanist 521 by
Flagholme Publishing Services.
Printed and made in Great Britain by CPI Group (UK) Ltd,
Croydon, CR0 4YY

Acknowledgements

Legislation is reproduced either courtesy of The National Archives or The Intellectual Property Office. This is indicated either as *The National Archives, 2015* for content from legislation.gov.uk (The National Archives, 2015 Crown Copyright licensed under the Open Government Licence, www.nationalarchives.gov.uk/doc/open-government-licence/version/3) or as *IPO, 2014* for material from *Unofficial consolidation of the CDPA 1988* by the Intellectual Property Office, 2014 (www.gov.uk/government/uploads/system/uploads/attachment_data/file/308729/cdpa1988-unofficial.pdf).

I would like to thank Ruth MacMullen for reading through a draft of the book, and providing feedback, comments and suggested improvements to the text.

As a member of LACA - the Libraries and Archives Copyright Alliance - since 1998, I also want to acknowledge how this has helped me develop my knowledge of copyright. The LACA membership brings together copyright experts across what some might refer to as the 'GLAM' sector, namely galleries, libraries, archives and museums.

Paul Pedley

Disclaimer

Paul Pedley is not a lawyer and is not able to give legal advice. The contents of this book do not constitute legal advice and should not be relied upon in that way.

Contents

Note: Sections of this book are cross-referred in the text with a capital S, e.g. 'see Section 2.1.1'. References to sections of Acts of Parliament and other laws use a lower-case s, e.g. 'see section 35' or 'see s 35' [of the Copyright, Designs and Patents Act 1988].

List of figures and tables

Figures

Tables

Table of statutes, etc.

Acts of Parliament

Statutory Instruments

International treaties and conventions

European Regulations

European Directives

Table of cases

Abbreviations

ALCS	Authors' Licensing and Collecting Society
ARROW	Accessible Registries of Rights Information and Orphan Works
BBC	British Broadcasting Corporation
BECS	British Equity Collecting Society Ltd
CC0	Creative Commons Zero (works which are free of copyright restrictions)
CDPA	Copyright, Designs and Patents Act 1988
CILIP	Chartered Institute of Library and Information Professionals
CLA	Copyright Licensing Agency
CJEU	Court of Justice of the European Union (sometimes referred to as the ECJ – the European Court of Justice)
CMO	collective management organization
DACS	Design and Artists Copyright Society
DRM	digital rights management
DVD	digital versatile disk
ECJ	European Court of Justice (see also CJEU)
EIDR	Entertainment Identifier Registry (a unique identifier for movie and television assets)
EIFL	Electronic Information for Libraries
ERA	Educational Recording Agency
EWCA	England and Wales Court of Appeal (law reports)
EWHC	England and Wales High Court (law reports)
EWPCC	England and Wales Patent County Court
IPIC	[Washington Treaty on] Intellectual Property in Respect of Integrated Circuits
IPO	Intellectual Property Office
ISAN	International Standard Audiovisual Number
ISBD	International Standard Bibliographic Description
ISBN	International Standard Book Number
ISMN	International Standard Music Numbering system

ISRC	International Standard Recording Code
ISSN	International Standard Serial Number
ISWC	International Standard Musical Work Code
MOOC	Massively Open Online Course
NLA	NLA Media Access (formerly known as the Newspaper Licensing Agency)
OHIM	Office for Harmonization in the Internal Market
PLS	Publishers Licensing Society
PPL	Phonographic Performance Limited
PRCA	Public Relations Consultants Association
PRS	Performing Right Society
RCUK	Research Councils UK
s, ss	section, sections (of a statute)
TLIB	Treaty Proposal on Copyright Limitations and Exceptions for Libraries and Archives
TPM	technical protection measures
TRIPS	Trade Related Aspects of Intellectual Property Rights
UCC	Universal Copyright Convention
VIAF	Virtual International Authority File
VIPs	visually impaired persons
VLE	virtual learning environment
WATCH	Writers, Artists and Their Copyright Holders
WCT	WIPO Copyright Treaty
WIPO	World Intellectual Property Organization
WPPT	WIPO Performances and Phonograms Treaty
WTO	World Trade Organization
WWW	World Wide Web

Glossary of terms

Acquis communautaire – the accumulated body of European Union law.

Commercial purpose – The legislation doesn't define 'commercial purpose'. The European Court of Justice has the final say. The test is whether the research is for a commercial purpose, not whether it is done by a commercial body (see the wording of recital 42 of the Copyright Directive 2001/29/EC).

Copyleft – the term 'copyleft' refers to the practice of making a work freely available, where there is a requirement for all modified and extended versions of the work to be freely available in the same way.

Copyright *acquis* – the body of copyright law of the European Union.

Derogatory treatment – is when the treatment of a work amounts to distortion or mutilation of the work, or is otherwise prejudicial to the honour or reputation of the author or director.

Disabled person – (for the purposes of the copyright exceptions in sections 31A–31BB of the CDPA 1988) means a person who has a physical or mental impairment which prevents the person from enjoying a copyright work to the same degree as a person who does not have that impairment, and 'disability' is to be construed accordingly (see CDPA 1988 s31F).

Educational establishment – (the meaning of 'educational establishment' for the purposes of the copyright exceptions is set out in a series of descriptions which can be found in the schedule to SI 2005/223.)

Embedded works – A copyright-protected work may include other works within it. If, for example, a book includes photographs, these will have their own separate rights.

Exhaustion – the principle of 'exhaustion' provides that a copyright owner's right to control copies of their work 'exhausts' on its first sale. So, for example, if someone were to buy a copy of a paperback book they would be at liberty to sell that to a second-hand book dealer. However, this principle does not automatically translate across into the digital sphere (see Section 5.9).

Fair dealing – a legal term which is used in order to establish whether a use of material protected by copyright is lawful, or whether it infringes copyright.

Industrial property – a useful way of collectively referring to patents, trade marks and designs, although the phrase is rarely used nowadays.

Judicial proceedings – includes proceedings before any court, tribunal or person having authority to decide any matter affecting a person's legal rights or liabilities.

Lending – means making a copy of the work available for use, on terms that it will or may be returned, otherwise than for direct or indirect economic or commercial advantage.

Library – in the context of the library exceptions means a library which is publicly accessible, or the library of an educational establishment; neither of these should be conducted for profit. Museums and galleries also benefit from the library exceptions. (The full definition can be found in s 43A, CDPA 1988.)

Made available to the public – means that the work has been made available by any means, including:

- the issue of copies to the public
- making the work available by means of an electronic retrieval system
- the rental or lending of copies of the work to the public
- the performance, exhibition, playing or showing of the work in public
- the communication to the public of the work.

Original – In order for a work to qualify for copyright protection it must be 'original', and whilst the term is not defined in the CDPA 1988, case law indicates that to qualify for protection it must be the result of the expenditure by the author of skill, judgement and experience, or labour, skill and capital.

Orphan work – is the term that has come to be used in order to describe a work where the rights holder is difficult or even impossible to identify or locate.

Parliamentary proceedings – 'includes proceedings of the Northern Ireland Assembly or of the Scottish Parliament or of the European Parliament and Assembly proceedings within the meaning of section 1(5) of the Government of Wales Act 2006'. (s 178, CDPA 1988)

Private study – does not include any study which is directly or indirectly for a commercial purpose.

Rental – means making a copy of the work available for use, on terms that it will or may be returned, for direct or indirect economic or commercial advantage.

Rights management information – means any information provided by the copyright owner or the holder of any right under copyright which identifies the work, the author, the copyright owner or the holder of any intellectual property rights, or information about the terms and conditions of use of the work, and any numbers or codes that represent such information.

Royal Commission – includes a Commission appointed for Northern Ireland by the Secretary of State in pursuance of the prerogative powers of Her Majesty delegated to him/her under section 7(2) of the Northern Ireland Constitution Act 1973.

Statutory inquiry – means an inquiry held or investigation conducted in pursuance of a duty imposed or power conferred by or under an enactment.

Substantial part – the term is not defined in copyright law. It isn't just a question of quantity, but also of quality. The phrase has been interpreted by the courts to mean a qualitatively significant part of a work even where this is not a large part of the work in terms of quantity.

Sufficient acknowledgement – an acknowledgement identifying the work in question by its title or other description, and identifying the author unless:

- in the case of a published work, it is published anonymously
- in the case of an unpublished work, it is not possible for a person to ascertain the identity of the author by reasonable inquiry.

Introduction

Copyright is an issue which information professionals ignore at their peril. They need to be aware of the potential risks and their consequences, and how those risks can be minimized. The problem is: how do they keep up to date with the law, and what aspects of copyright law are of most relevance to them?

Keeping up to date with copyright law can be very time-consuming. I invest a lot of time in monitoring copyright developments in the UK, Europe and beyond (such as initiatives from WIPO, the World Intellectual Property Organization). And indeed, now that the UK's copyright legislation has had a significant overhaul, the focus has switched to European and wider international developments. This book is a distillation of the knowledge that I have built up, and it will hopefully be of benefit to people who aren't able to monitor dozens of RSS feeds, Twitter feeds, blogs and the like covering copyright on a daily basis.

It is only on very rare occasions that copyright law can be considered to be a matter of black and white. Instead it is often a matter of opinion. This book reflects my understanding of the law. It is important to bear in mind that I am not a lawyer, and that what it contains does not constitute legal advice. The book aims to be a core text for library and information professionals, covering the copyright issues which are of the greatest importance for carrying out their day-to-day work. In view of the many changes to copyright law that took place in 2014 it is important for practitioners to be able to refer to an up-to-date text.

During the course of 2014 a number of significant amendments were made to the Copyright, Designs and Patents Act 1988: important changes were made to the copyright exceptions and a number of measures were introduced to help address the problem of how to use orphan works legitimately.

The changes to the copyright exceptions will undoubtedly be of benefit to many librarians:

- The vast majority of the copyright exceptions could previously be overridden by contracts and licences, whereas now many – but certainly not all – of the exceptions have clauses within them which expressly forbid contract override.

- There was a lack of certainty around copyright declaration forms and the use of electronic signatures, whereas now a signature isn't required and the forms can be completed electronically.

The extent to which libraries, museums and archives are able to benefit from the changes to the copyright exceptions will in many ways be dependent upon their attitude towards risk. Here are some examples of how libraries and museums have made use of the new or amended exceptions:

- A national library has provided sound recordings to individuals who aren't able-bodied and who are unable to visit in person.
- A number of libraries in the higher education sector are now content-mining sound recordings.
- A national museum has used the dedicated terminals exception to provide access to digitized papers which are too fragile to be displayed.
- Museums are using the preservation exception to make digital copies of their collection items.
- The library of a musical conservatoire has used the illustration for instruction exception to reproduce excerpts of sheet music and audio tracks and upload these to the VLE.
- A number of libraries have been receiving copyright declaration forms electronically, which has been of particular benefit to distance learners.

Who is this book for?

The book has been written primarily for library and information professionals, regardless of sector. It will also be relevant for students on information-related courses, as well as for authors and publishers who are interested in how library and information staff use their works. The book has been written primarily with people in the United Kingdom in mind. But it will also be of interest to librarians in Europe, and common law countries such as the USA, Australia, Canada and New Zealand.

The most likely use of the book is as a point of reference for librarians to be able to look up a particular topic and to see what the book says about that particular issue (such as mass digitization of copyright-protected works, embedding, e-book lending, or the extent to which publicly accessible libraries can rely on the exception for making available content on dedicated terminals).

★ Throughout the book, particularly useful resources are highlighted with shading and a star in the margin, thus.

The book contains an index, a glossary of terms, a list of abbreviations, and listings of relevant legislation and case law. It also has quite a few figures and tables which try to summarize the key points on topics such as the copyright implications of MOOCs, how digital rights management systems affect libraries, the interface between copyright exceptions and licences, a summary of the educational exceptions and key points about 'commercial purpose' and about the meaning of 'substantial'.

What is covered?

The main body of the book consists of eight chapters:

Chapter 1 – General principles
Chapter 2 – Legislative framework
Chapter 3 – The copyright exceptions
Chapter 4 – Licensing
Chapter 5 – Digital copyright
Chapter 6 – Orphan works
Chapter 7 – Copyright compliance
Chapter 8 – Copyright for the corporate sector.

The first two chapters serve to set the scene – Chapter 1 sets out the basics of copyright, while Chapter 2 outlines the various component parts which together make up the legislative framework within which we operate.

In order to copy material people need permission, and this can be achieved either through the use of a copyright exception or through having a licence in place, and so there are separate chapters on each of those topics. Together, Chapters 3 and 4 could be said to form the core of the book. Chapter 3 looks in depth at the copyright exceptions. It draws out the points of most relevance to library and information professionals. Chapter 4 looks at the use of copyright licences to cover copying activities where it isn't possible to rely on a copyright exception.

Chapter 5, on digital copyright, examines issues which are relevant to the use of content in the digital world. For example, it considers the exclusive right to communicate a work to the public as the right only applies to communicating a work to the public by electronic means. Drawing upon relevant case law it looks at topics such as the use of hyperlinks as well as the embedding of content, archiving and preservation of digital content, mass digitization, digital goods and the exhaustion of rights, as well as rental and lending of digital content.

Chapter 6 runs through the available solutions for copying orphan works: one solution is free of charge in the form of an exception that covers the copying of orphan works by publicly accessible libraries. Another solution has a price-tag attached, namely the use of licences. And the cost of a licence depends upon the type of the intended usage – whether it be for a commercial or a non-commercial purpose. The chapter considers how these solutions work in practice, and the boundaries or limits on the extent to which these solutions can be relied upon.

Chapter 7 looks at copyright compliance. Staying within the law is both a legal and also an ethical issue for information professionals. The chapter considers topics such as what constitutes an infringement of copyright, how copyright should be considered as a matter of risk management and how different copying activities need to be graded according to level of risk. Another important topic considered in the chapter relates to liability – who would be liable for an infringement of copyright: would it, for example, be the employing institution who would be pursued or an individual librarian? The chapter also looks at how to trace rights owners and describes the copyright clearance process. It also considers what happens when things go wrong, and in particular the question of dispute resolution.

Information professionals working in the corporate sector are very constrained in terms of what they can copy under the copyright exceptions, and this is true for a number of reasons. For example, a number of the exceptions limit the copying to where it is being done for a non-commercial purpose; there are a number of exceptions which are only available for the benefit of publicly accessible, not-for-profit libraries. I have written Chapter 8 specifically for corporate information professionals, because of the particular difficulties that they face.

What is not covered

One topic which isn't covered by the book is open access. To do it justice, one could write an entire book about open access. It is of most relevance to the academic sector, and because I don't work in the academic sector I believe that copyright experts working at universities and further education colleges would be able to write about open access in a more informed way, and could do so far better than myself.

Paul Pedley

CHAPTER 1

General principles

This chapter runs through the basics of UK copyright law and equips the reader with a framework for analysing copyright problems. The chapter covers:

1.1   What copyright is (1.1)
1.2   What copyright protects (1.2)
1.3   How one obtains copyright protection (1.3)
1.4   How long copyright lasts (1.4)
1.5   Copyright ownership (1.5)
1.6   Who is an 'author'? (1.6)
1.7   Economic and moral rights (1.7)
1.8   How copyright fits within the wider range of intellectual property rights (1.8)
1.9   A framework for analysing copyright problems (1.9).

1.1   What copyright is

Copyright protects the works of authors and performers for a specific period of time. During the period that the protection is in place, the owner of the rights in a work is able to exploit the work in any way they wish.

Copyright isn't a single right, but is instead a whole bundle of rights that are given to the creators of various types of works. It includes, for example, reproduction right, the right of communication to the public and the right to make an adaptation or translation of the work.

Copyright is intended to encourage and stimulate the creation of works by writers, artists, dramatists, musicians, photographers, film producers and so on by providing safeguards which protect and reward their creativity.

One might think of copyright as a negative right, because it is the right to prevent other people from copying the work.

1.2   What copyright protects

In order for a work to be protected by copyright it must be:

1 original
2 fixed
3 one of the types of works that are given protection (see 1.2.3)
4 by a UK citizen, or have had its first publication in the UK (see a fuller
   explanation at 1.2.4).

1.2.1   Original

The word 'original' is not defined in the Copyright, Designs and Patents Act 1988. However, case law helps to clarify what is meant by the word 'original'. Phrases that have been used by judges in various copyright cases[1] to explain the requirement of originality show that to qualify for protection it must be the result of the expenditure by the author of skill, judgement and experience, or labour, skill and capital. There is, however, a definition of the word 'original' with regard to a database, and that can be found in the CDPA 1988 section 3A:

> a literary work consisting of a database is original if, and only if, by reason of the
> selection or arrangement of the contents of the database the database constitutes the
> author's own intellectual creation
>
> National Archives, 2015

1.2.2   Fixed

Copyright does not protect ideas. It only protects works which have been expressed in a material form. In other words, copyright protects works where they have been fixed in a form that makes it possible for them to be copied. If, for example, someone has the idea of taking a picture of a sunset they cannot use copyright law to protect the idea as such. However, if they were to take a picture from their back bedroom window of the sun setting, that specific picture would be protected.

1.2.3   The types of work that are protected

Copyright protects works that can be categorized as being one of the following:

- literary works
- dramatic works
- musical works
- artistic works

- sound recordings
- films
- broadcasts.

Copyright law only protects works where they fit within these categories. In the case of software, for example, copyright protects an author's original expression in a computer program as a 'literary work'. The source code can therefore be viewed as a human-readable literary work, which expresses the ideas of the software engineers who authored it. Not only the human-readable instructions (source code) but also binary machine-readable instructions (object code) are considered to be literary works or 'written expressions', and are therefore also protected.

In addition to the categories or species listed above, copyright also protects the typographical arrangement of published editions. Copying the typographic arrangement would involve making a facsimile copy of the page layout or arrangement.

1.2.4   UK nationality, domicile or residence or first publication in the UK

In order for a work to be protected under the UK's copyright laws, the author's nationality, domicile or residence must be in the UK or else the work must have been first published in the UK (this would include where it has been simultaneously published elsewhere within 30 days). The legal requirements regarding authorship are set out in section 154 of the CDPA 1988. As a result of the UK's commitments under international agreements such as the Berne Convention for the Protection of Literary and Artistic Works 1886 the UK does protect the works of authors from other countries (see the last paragraph of Section 1.3 below).

1.3   How one obtains copyright protection

Copyright is automatic. As soon as a work is created and meets the requirements for protection (that it is original, that it is fixed in a material form, that it is by a British citizen or was first published in the UK, and that it fits into the protected categories or species) the work will automatically be protected by UK copyright law. This is one of the fundamental differences between copyright and 'industrial property' (a collective term which has fallen out of regular use, but which refers to patents, trade marks and designs). In the case of copyright the protection arises automatically and there is no registration process involved. Indeed, compulsory registration would contravene the Berne Convention of 1886, which is the main instrument governing copyright at an international level, whereas in the case of industrial property the rights have to be applied for. With industrial property the completion of a registration process is normally required, along with payment of a fee in order to receive protection.

The other major difference between copyright and industrial property rights relates to international protection. In the case of patents, trade and service marks, and design rights, one applies for protection in one country – in this case it would be protection within the UK. In the case of patents, there is no such thing as a single international or worldwide patent. Normally it is necessary to file separate patent applications in each of the countries for which protection is sought. However, there are a number of systems which help to make the process of applying for protection in multiple countries as efficient as possible. These include the filing of an international Patent Cooperation Treaty patent application or a European patent application; and it will soon be possible to apply for patent protection throughout most of the European Union using the Unified Patent system.

In the case of copyright a work is automatically protected around the world as a result of the Berne Convention, which has as one of its main principles the idea of mutual protection. Each of the Berne Union's 168 member countries is required to protect works from other countries to the same level as it protects works originating in its own country. This is sometimes referred to as the principle of national treatment.

Part I of the Copyright, Designs and Patents Act 1988 confers copyright on the creators of certain works. Part II of the Act confers rights on performers and persons having recording rights in relation to a performance. The performances that are protected by performance right are dramatic performances, musical performances, readings or recitations of literary works and the performance of a variety act. It means that anyone other than the performer who holds the rights requires their consent in order to exploit the performances. This means that live performances are protected, as are broadcasts of the performance and other recordings of the performance.

There is a statutory instrument which deals with the protection of works from other countries. The protection depends on which countries are signed up to the international treaties and conventions, most notably the Berne Convention; and as a result a new statutory instrument is published every so often containing a consolidated list of the countries to which the reciprocal protection provisions apply. The current statutory instrument covering the protection of works from other countries is The Copyright and Performances (Application to Other Countries) Order 2013: SI 2013/536 as amended by the Copyright and Performances (Application to Other Countries) (Amendment) Order 2015: SI 2015/216. However, if section 22 of the Intellectual Property Act 2014 on recognition of foreign copyright works and performances is brought into force it will amend sections 154 and 155 of the CDPA 1988 and will provide for the automatic extension of certain copyright provisions of the CDPA to nationals of, and works first published in, other countries without the need to include an extensive list of countries and territories in an order. The section inserts references to a large number of those countries and territories into the body of the CDPA wherever relevant. In many cases protection will automatically extend to new signatory states without the need for a new order to implement the UK's obligations under the relevant treaty.

1.4   How long copyright lasts

If anyone were to ask how long copyright lasts that may seem a straightforward question, but as with so many areas of copyright law, the answer isn't quite as straightforward as the question might at first suggest. The rule of thumb is that copyright lasts for the lifetime of the author plus 70 years. This is true not just for the UK but also for the rest of the European Economic Area, which consists of the 28 member states that form the European Union plus Norway, Iceland and Liechtenstein.

When calculating the date of copyright expiry a point to bear in mind is that the date on which copyright ends isn't 70 years after the precise date on which the author died, but is rather 31 December of the 70th year after the year in which the author died. So if an author died on 15 March 1956, the copyright would expire on 31 December 2026.

There are some exceptions to copyright lasting for the life of the author plus 70 years. They include:

- Crown and parliamentary material: where the work has been published commercially copyright lasts for 50 years from date of creation; and in the case of Crown material, for works which haven't been published commercially copyright lasts for 125 years from the end of the calendar year in which the work was made
- typographical arrangement of published editions: 25 years from the end of the calendar year in which the edition was first published
- computer-generated works: 50 years from the end of the calendar year in which the work was made
- broadcasts: 50 years from the end of the calendar year in which the broadcast was made
- unpublished literary, dramatic and musical works which were still unpublished when the CDPA 1988 came into force in 1989 are in copyright until 2039.

The lifetimes of copyright protection for various categories of work are summarized in Table 1.1.

At the end of October 2014 the government published a consultation on reducing the duration of copyright in certain unpublished works and the 2039 rule

Table 1.1 *Lifetimes of copyright protection*

Category	Materials included in category	Lifetime of copyright protection
Literary works	Written works. Includes lyrics, tables, compilations, computer programs, letters, memoranda and e-mails.	Author's life plus 70 years after death.
Dramatic works	Plays, works of dance and mime, and also the libretto of an opera.	Author's life plus 70 years after death.
Musical works	Musical scores.	Author's life plus 70 years after death.
Artistic works	Paintings, drawings, diagrams, maps, charts, plans, engravings, etchings, lithographs, woodcuts, photographs, sculptures, collages, architectural works and works of artistic craftsmanship.	Author's/creator's life plus 70 years after death.
Computer -generated works	Literary, dramatic and musical works.	50 years from the end of the calendar year in which the work was made.
Databases	Collections of independent works, data or other materials which (a) are arranged in a systematic or methodical way, or (b) are individually accessible by electronic or other means.	Full term of other relevant copyrights in the material. In addition, there is a database right for 15 years where a substantial investment has been made in the selection and arrangement of the contents of the database; and a further substantial investment would trigger another 15-year period of protection.
Sound recordings	Regardless of medium or the device on which they are played.	The length of term of copyright in a sound recording depends on whether or not it has been published (released) or has been communicated to the public (for example, played on the radio): • If a recording is not published or communicated to the public, copyright lasts for 50 years from when the recording was made. • If a recording is published within 50 years of when it was made, copyright lasts for 70 years from the year it was first published. • If a recording is not published within 50 years of when it was made, but it is communicated to the public, copyright lasts for 70 years from the year it was first communicated to the public. • If a recording is first communicated to the public within 50 years of when it was made and is then published at a later date (but within 70 years of its first communication to the public), copyright lasts for 70 years from the year it was first published.

Table 1.1 *(Continued)*		
Category	**Materials included in category**	**Lifetime of copyright protection**
Films	Any medium from which a moving image may be reproduced.	70 years from death of whoever is the last to survive from: principal director, author of dialogue, composer of film music.
Broadcasts	An electronic transmission of visual images, sounds or other information (see CDPA 1988 s6).	50 years from when broadcast first made.
Published editions	The typography and layout of a literary, dramatic or musical work.	25 years from first publication.
Crown copyright	All works 'made by Her Majesty or by an officer or servant of the Crown in the course of his [or her] duties' (s 163, CDPA 1988).	Published work: 50 years from the end of the year when first published. Unpublished work: 125 years beyond the year in which the work was created.
Parliamentary copyright	Works made by or under the direction or control of the House of Commons or House of Lords.	50 years from the end of the calendar year in which the work was made.

see www.gov.uk/government/consultations/reducing-the-duration-of-copyright-in-certain-unpublished-works. Some very old unpublished works are still protected by copyright in the UK, even though their authors may have died hundreds of years previously. In 2013 Parliament approved powers to remove these complex rules so as to reduce the duration of copyright in certain unpublished works. However, the IPO did not implement the proposed changes to the term of protection during the first quarter of 2015 as planned. This was on human rights grounds – specifically relating to the protection of property, which is set out in Article 1 of the European Convention on Human Rights. The article says that 'Every natural or legal person is entitled to the peaceful enjoyment of his possessions. No one shall be deprived of his possessions except in the public interest and subject to the conditions provided for by law and by the general principles of international law.' Reducing the copyright term from 2039 to life plus 70 would deprive rights holders of income which they were expecting to continue to receive until 2039.

1.5 Copyright ownership

In general, the author of a work is the first owner of any copyright in it.

Where the work is made by an employee in the course of his/her employment, the employer is the first owner of any copyright in the work, in the absence of a written agreement to the contrary. This only applies to employees, not to contractors, so the mere fact that a work has been commissioned and paid for does not give the ownership of the copyright to the commissioning party. So, if an employee on behalf of his or her company were to pay an external consultant to write a report, the mere fact that the consultant has been paid doesn't mean that the consultant is no longer the holder of the copyright in that report. Copyright issues need to be thought through right from the outset, before any commissioning contract is signed. It is advisable for a clause in the commissioning agreement with the external consultant to be included where they agree to either transfer the copyrights in any outputs from the commissioned work to the company who are paying for the work to be done or alternatively to license the commissioning company to use the work in a number of different ways, such as to be able to load a copy of the report onto its organizational intranet.

It is also worth bearing in mind that copyright is an intellectual 'property' right, and that property ownership is subject to change. For example, the rights could be sold and/or signed over to someone else. This is an important point to take into account when one is trying to trace a rights holder – the first owner of copyright is not necessarily the current owner.

1.6   Who is an 'author'?

'Author', in relation to a work, means the person who creates it. That person shall be taken to be:

- for sound recordings – the producer
- for films – the producer and the principal director
- for broadcasts – the person making the broadcast
- for computer-generated literary, dramatic, musical or artistic works – the person by whom the arrangements necessary for the creation of the work are undertaken.

If the identity of the author is unknown – and cannot be ascertained by reasonable inquiry – or, in the case of a work of joint authorship, none of the authors is known, then these are taken to be works of **unknown authorship.** Where a work is produced by the collaboration of two or more authors in which the contribution of each author is not distinct from that of the other author or authors, then these are known as works of **joint authorship.**

1.7   Economic and moral rights

The author, as first owner of copyright in the work, has a number of exclusive rights. These can be grouped into economic rights and moral rights. The economic rights consist of the following rights:

- to copy the work
- to issue copies of the work to the public
- to rent or lend the work to the public
- to perform, show or play the work in public
- to communicate the work to the public
- to make an adaptation of the work or to do any of the above in relation to an adaptation.

Copyright is not one right but is instead a bundle of rights which includes the distribution right, the reproduction right and the exclusive right to communicate the work to the public by electronic means. It is important to remember this when undertaking rights clearance, as there may be more than one rights holder involved.

The rights owner has the exclusive right to exploit each of the economic rights, and if anyone other than the rights owner undertakes any of the protected activities without permission, that would constitute a primary infringement. It isn't necessarily the case that anyone wishing to get the required permission to copy the work would have to approach the rights holder directly. Permission can take a number of different forms:

- a copyright exception or permitted act set out in the CDPA 1988 could provide the required permission
- a licence from a collecting society which has been given a mandate by the rights owner to act on their behalf
- or, it could be the written permission of the rights holder.

In addition to the economic rights, the author has four moral rights (section numbers are from the Copyright, Designs and Patents Act 1988):

1 the right of paternity, ss 77–79
2 the right of integrity, s 80
3 the right to object to false attribution, s 84
4 the right to privacy s 85.

The **right of paternity**, as set out in sections 77–79 of the CDPA 1988, is the right of the author to be identified as such. This right cannot be infringed unless the author has asserted his/her right to be identified as the author of the work. This is why within the first few pages of a book there will often be a form of words along the lines 'Joe Bloggs asserts his right to be identified as the author of this work'. The publishing contract between the author and a commercial publisher should also contain a clause setting out how the right of paternity will be asserted. There are a number of exceptions to the paternity right. For example, it does not apply to computer programs, designs of typefaces and computer-generated works.

Nor does it apply to works generated in the course of employment.

The **right of integrity**, as set out in section 80 of the CDPA 1988, is the right of the author to prevent or object to derogatory treatment of his/her work. This is especially relevant in the electronic environment, where it is easy to manipulate images or text in art or word-processing packages.

The **right to object to false attribution**, as set out in section 84 of the CDPA 1988, is the right of persons not to have a literary, dramatic, musical or artistic work falsely attributed to them, nor to have a film falsely attributed to them as the director.

The **right to privacy**, as set out in section 85 of the CDPA 1988, is the right of the author to withhold certain photographs or films from publication. Under the UK Act this would apply to a person who commissions the work but decides not to have it issued to the public, exhibited or shown in public.

Moral rights can be waived in writing; however, they cannot be assigned or transferred. But the rights of paternity, integrity and privacy can be 'willed' to someone.

In the consultation paper on taking forward the Gowers recommendations on the copyright exceptions[2] the IPO says:

> The UK's legislation contains enforceable moral rights provisions but other options, such as passing off, trade mark infringement, or an action for injurious falsehood may be used to protect business reputations and an action for defamation may also be used to protect the reputation of an individual.

Computer programs are excluded from the moral right to be identified as the author (section 77) or the moral right to object to a derogatory treatment of a work (section 80).

1.8 How copyright fits within the wider range of intellectual property rights

There are four main types of intellectual property:

1 patents
2 trade marks
3 design right
4 copyright.

In addition, there are a few other areas of law which are relevant: the law of 'passing off' and the law of confidence, which covers both confidential information and privacy. An action for breach of confidence can be used in order to protect trade secrets and government secrets and also to protect personal secrets.

1.8.1   Patents

Patents are for inventions, new and improved products and processes that are capable of industrial application and which involve an inventive step. Patents have to be applied for. They are costly to obtain and especially to maintain if they are renewed for the full period of protection, with the renewal fees increasing yearly throughout the lifetime of the patent. Their maximum lifetime is 20 years from the date when the patent was first applied for. In order to be patentable an idea must be:

- **New** – not already in the public domain or the subject of a previous patent.
- **Non-obvious** – it should not be common sense to any accomplished practitioner in the field who having been asked to solve a particular practical problem would see this solution immediately. That is to say, it should not be self-evident using available skills or technologies.

and

- **Useful**, or applicable in industry – it must have a stated function, and could immediately be produced to fulfil this function.

Software is protected by copyright, and potentially it could be protected by a patent, but only where it consists of something more than a computer program, as was the case in Symbian Ltd v Comptroller General of Patents [2008] EWCA Civ 1066, where it was held that a substantive technical contribution was made. To determine whether there is a technical contribution, ask whether:

- technical means are used to produce a result or solve a problem, or
- the invention produces a technical result.

1.8.2   Trade and service marks

Trade and service marks are for brand identity of goods and services, and having trade marks allows distinctions to be made between them. Trade marks fall into two types – registered and unregistered. Registered trade marks involve a formal application procedure with associated fees and renewal fees which makes it easier to take legal action against infringers. Unregistered trade marks involve no such procedures or costs, but provide less robust protection. Trade marks are typically a symbol, image or word (although they can in some circumstances be a shape, a colour or a combination of these) that is associated with particular goods or services provided by the owner. Both types of mark can last indefinitely so long as the owner still actively uses them and, in the case of a registered trade mark, that the renewal fees are paid. The owner of a registered trade mark has the right to take legal action to prevent third parties from using their mark (or something deceptively similar) in the course of trade. In the case of an unregistered trade mark, if the owner of a mark found that someone else was using their mark without permission, they would need to use the common law of 'passing off' in order to take action against them. To be successful in a passing off action, you would have to prove that:

1   the mark is yours
2   you have built up a reputation in the mark
3   you have been harmed in some way by the other person's use of the mark.

1.8.3   Design right

Design right covers the appearance of the whole or part of a product resulting from the features of, the lines, contours, colour, shape, texture and materials of the product itself and its ornamentation. The right can last for up to 25 years from the date of filing in the case of registered designs, and will need to be renewed every five years. In the case of unregistered designs, the design right automatically protects designs for 10 years after the design was first sold or 15 years after it was created, whichever is earliest.

1.8.4   Copyright

Copyright protects works such as literary, dramatic, and artistic material, music, films, sound recordings and broadcasts. Within copyright there are, as we have already seen in Section 1.7, a series of economic and moral rights, and there are also a number of 'neighbouring rights' (rights outside copyright but which are related to it, such as performance rights).

1.9   A framework for analysing copyright problems

Copyright can be a complex topic. In order to avoid feeling overwhelmed by copyright questions it is useful to break things down into a number of component parts, and to consider each of these in turn. If you are faced with a copyright query in your role as an information professional, you can use the questions set out in Figure 1.1 to consider the essential issues.

It may very well seem as though these four points are stating the obvious. But they can be used as a step-by-step approach to analyse copyright problems. It is important to work through the questions one at a time in the order

1   Is the work protected by copyright?
2   Is there a copyright exception that covers my intended use of the work?
3   Is there a licence available that would cover my intended use?
4   Do I need to get permission from the rights owner for my intended use of the work?

Figure 1.1
A framework for analysing copyright problems

shown in Figure 1.1, as each subsequent step follows on logically from the previous one. Working through each of the questions one by one will ensure that you have systematically considered the essential points that are required for solving copyright problems.

1.9.1   Is the work protected by copyright?

The first question asks whether the work to be copied is protected by copyright and therefore requires permission to copy from it, or whether the work is part of the public domain and as a result no longer subject to the restrictions of copyright.

Copyright does not protect facts, ideas, numbers or names; although a collection of facts could potentially be protected by database right.

The reference to the term 'public domain' relates to where a work has either been through its period of copyright protection, and is now no longer protected by copyright, or to a work which the rights owner has chosen to mark as being public domain.

To decide whether a particular work is now out of copyright it is necessary to think through the period of protection that applies to that particular work. The normal rule of thumb is 'life of the author plus 70 years', but bear in mind situations where the period of protection differs from the normal rule of thumb:

- Crown and parliamentary material, 50 years from date of creation
- published editions (typography), 25 years from first publication
- computer-generated works, 50 years from first creation.

There are a number of tools available to help people establish whether a work is in the public domain. Figure 1.2 lists a couple of examples.

Even if the work would still be within copyright, the next question to ask is whether the rights holder has marked the work with a public domain symbol. The Creative Commons movement has a CC0 (CC Zero) symbol (Figure 1.3 on the next page). This is a tool which

- http://outofcopyright.eu (the Europeana public domain calculator)
- www.calculateurdomainepublic.fr (a public domain calculator provided through a partnership between the Open Knowledge Foundation France and the French Ministry of Culture and Communication)

Figure 1.2
Tools for identifying if a work is in the public domain

enables the rights owner to free their work of copyright restrictions around the world. It can be used even if the work is free of copyright in some jurisdictions in order to make sure that it is treated as being free of copyright everywhere. (Section 4.10 looks at the Creative Commons licences in more detail.)

The CC0 symbol allows copyright holders to place works in the public domain to the extent legally possible, worldwide. Rights holders can waive all of their

Figure 1.3
*Public domain symbol (Work found at
https://creativecommons.org/about/downloads. Licensed under a
Creative Commons Attribution 4.0 international licence
https://creativecommons.org/licences/by/4.0)*

copyrights and related or neighbouring rights, including their moral rights, to the extent that these can be waived.

You would need to be confident that where the CC0 symbol is given on a work that it has been placed there by the rights holder, or with their permission. An individual cannot waive rights to a work either that they do not own or where they do not have the permission of the owner.

It is important to distinguish between public domain and what is publicly accessible. There is often a perception, especially in view of the considerable body of material that is available on the internet, that anything which is publicly accessible can be copied and used without restriction. Researchers may well try to justify their copying on the basis that a work is available on the web and there is no copyright symbol on the work and no copyright statement on the website. But copyright is automatic, and so even if the rights owner hasn't put a copyright statement on their work, if it is original, fixed, and fits into the various categories that are protected by copyright law, then it will have the protections of copyright law.

1.9.2   Is there a copyright exception that covers my intended use of the work?

If you have established that the work you wish to copy from is still protected by copyright, the next step would be to think through whether your intended use of the work would be covered by one of the copyright exceptions or permitted acts. The main copyright exceptions used by library and information professionals are considered in detail in Chapter 3. Even if there is an exception available it may be that your intended use still falls outside the scope of the permitted act you were thinking of, because of something qualifying or limiting the scope of the exception, for example where:

- it only covers use for a non-commercial purpose; or
- it only covers use by publicly accessible libraries, archives, museums, galleries and the libraries of educational establishments that are not for profit; or
- it is only available where the use would be considered to be fair dealing.

All of the copyright exceptions are subject to a three-step test:

1   only applies in special cases
2   doesn't conflict with a normal exploitation of the work, and
3   doesn't unreasonably prejudice the legitimate interests of the rights holder.

The three-step test comes from Article 9 of the Berne Convention, and also appears in Article 5(5) of the Copyright Directive (2001/29/EU, also known as the 'InfoSoc' Directive).

1.9.3   Is there a licence that covers my use?

Where your intended use of the work is not covered by one of the copyright exceptions, the next step would be to consider whether a licence agreement would provide the solution. Licence agreements may allow you to use a work for one or more specified purposes and may apply only for a limited time or in specific places. A number of different types of copyright licence are available. They include:

- licences from collective licensing societies such as the Copyright Licensing Agency, NLA Media Access, the Educational Recording Agency or the Performing Right Society.
- an orphan works licence. In October 2014 a licensing regime for the use of orphan works was introduced. This could be a licence directly from the Intellectual Property Office, or in due course it is anticipated that there will be licences available through collecting societies where they have been authorized by the IPO to operate an orphan works licence for a particular category of material.
- a Creative Commons licence (see Figure 1.4). As there are a number of different Creative Commons licences available, it is important to check whether the licence terms covering the work you have in mind would cover your intended use. For example, are you planning to use the work for a commercial purpose, because not all of the Creative Commons licences allow this.
- one of the licences available within the UK Government Licensing Framework: the main licence under the government licensing framework is the Open Government Licence, but there is also a non-commercial government licence, and a Charged Licence; or
- the Open Parliament Licence.

Chapter 4 explores copyright licensing in more detail (see Section 4.10 for Creative Commons licences).

Attribution (CC BY)
Attribution No Derivatives (CC BY ND)
Attribution Non Commercial Share Alike (CC BY NC SA)
Attribution Share Alike (CC BY SA)
Attribution Non Commercial (CC BY NC)
Attribution Non Commercial No Derivatives (CC BY NC ND)

Figure 1.4 *Creative Commons licence types*

1.9.4   Do I need permission from the copyright owner for my use?

Having worked through the first three questions, the final point to consider is whether it is necessary to contact the rights holder directly in order to get their permission to copy the work.

As part of the process of getting permission from the rights holder, ask the following questions:

- Have I got the permission in writing?
- Have I got permission from the right person?
- And have they provided a warranty and an indemnity to back up the assertion that they are indeed the rights owner?

Chapter 7 on copyright compliance covers the process of getting permission from the copyright holder in more detail.

Notes

1   Cases which explore the meaning of 'original' include Ladbroke v William Hill [1964] 1 All ER 465, Macmillan v Cooper (1923) 93 LJPC and Interlego v Tyco [1988] RPC 343.

2   Intellectual Property Office (2007) *Taking Forward the Gowers Review of Intellectual Property: proposed changes to copyright exceptions,* http://bufvc.ac.uk/copyright-guidance/mlr/index.php/site/436.

CHAPTER 2

Legislative framework

This chapter outlines the four components which form the legislative framework for UK copyright law. It is important to understand these various different elements in order to ensure compliance with copyright law because together they represent the legal framework within which library and information professionals, as well as copyright practitioners need to operate.

- It runs through the international treaties and conventions to which the UK is a party as well as highlighting a draft treaty (TLIB) which, if it were to be passed, would introduce a series of mandatory copyright exceptions (Section 2.1).
- It examines the body of European copyright law, including regulations and directives (Section 2.2)
- It looks at UK statute law, of which the CDPA 1988 (as amended) is the most significant (Section 2.3)
- It looks at the role of case law (Section 2.4)
- Finally it outlines information sources on EU and UK legislation and case law.

The chapter cites a number of websites for accessing the primary source materials (UK and EU legislation and case law, as well as a number of sources for wider international laws). It also cites websites which help with monitoring the progress of legislation as it goes through its parliamentary stages.

The legislative framework governing copyright in the UK is made up of a number of component parts. These are:

1 **International treaties and conventions** – the UK is signatory to a number of international agreements covering copyright, and is required to honour the obligations set out in those agreements.
2 **European directives, regulations and decisions** – as one of the 28 EU member states, the UK is required to implement the *acquis communautaire (*the 'copyright acquis'[1]), or the accumulated body of European Union law. This

consists of directives, regulations, and treaties[2], as well as the decisions of the European Court of Justice.

3 **UK statute law** in the form of Acts of Parliament and Statutory Instruments.

4 **Case law** to help us understand how the legislation applies in particular circumstances.

Bearing in mind the UK's European and wider international commitments, the UK government does not have a completely free hand when developing copyright law; and instead even if the UK parliament decides to initiate its own copyright laws (as opposed to merely transposing European directives or other international obligations into UK law) it has to ensure that it operates within the limits, constraints and boundaries that are set for the UK by those international obligations.

2.1   International treaties and conventions

The international copyright landscape is characterized by an emphasis on the protection of rights, with no reciprocal protection for the use of works. There is currently only one international agreement which has been signed and which protects exceptions and limitations, and that is the Marrakesh Treaty for the blind and visually impaired (see Section 2.1.5), and that hasn't yet come into force.

2.1.1   Berne Convention (1886)

The Berne Convention for the protection of literary and artistic works was the first international convention on copyright protection and was established in 1886. The Berne Convention has been revised a number of times since 1886, the last amendment being in 1979. The Berne Convention has 168 members, the most recent signatories to the convention being Lao People's Democratic Republic, Kuwait, Mozambique and Vanuatu. The Convention rests on three basic principles:

1 National treatment (mutual protection) – among Berne Union members, each state must protect the work of others to the same level as in their own country.

2 Automatic protection – no registration is required before protection is given. Protection is granted automatically and is not subject to the formality of registration, deposit or the like.

3 The principle of independence of protection – the protection is independent of the existence of protection in the country of origin of the work.

2.1.2   Universal Copyright Convention (1952)

The Universal Copyright Convention was agreed at a UNESCO conference in Geneva in 1952 and it established the copyright symbol of ©. The main features of the UCC are:

1 Works of a given country must carry a copyright notice to secure protection in other UCC countries – the internationally recognized © copyright symbol.
2 Foreign works must be treated as though they are national works.
3 There is a minimum period of protection – life plus 25 years.
4 The author's translation rights may be subjected to compulsory licensing.

The Berne Convention and the TRIPS Agreement (see Section 2.1.3) are arguably more significant than the Universal Copyright Convention, for a number of reasons. A key provision within the UCC is that the © symbol needs to be used in order to secure the various protections set out in the Universal Copyright Convention. But this is no longer relevant because, apart from Cambodia, all of the parties to the Universal Copyright Convention are also signed up to the Berne Convention, which makes clear that copyright protection is automatic without the need for any formalities. And as Cambodia is a member of the World Trade Organization, it is required to follow the provisions of the TRIPS Agreement, which also obliges it to comply with the Berne Convention (apart from the section on moral rights). A second reason why the UCC's features have limited significance is that it requires signatories to the agreement to ensure that copyright is protected for a minimum of life plus 25 years, whereas all of the countries involved are actually required under the Berne Convention to give copyright protection to works for a minimum of life plus 50 years.

2.1.3   Trade Related Aspects of Intellectual Property Rights (1994)

Another international instrument that deals with copyright is the TRIPS Agreement. TRIPS stands for Trade Related Aspects of Intellectual Property Rights. The TRIPS Agreement was signed in 1994 as an annex to the main World Trade Organization (WTO) agreement (to be precise, it is Annex 1C to 'The Final Act Embodying the Results of the Uruguay Round of Multilateral Trade Negotiations') and it came into effect on 1 January 1995. It is designed to ensure that intellectual property rights do not themselves become barriers to legitimate trade.

The WTO has 161 members. All members of the WTO are bound by the TRIPS Agreement, regardless of their levels of development. Pursuant to the TRIPS Agreement, WTO members must comply with the substantive law provisions of the Berne Convention and the Appendix except for the moral rights provisions of the Berne Convention, regardless of whether or not they are party to the Berne Convention.

A basic principle concerning the nature and scope of obligations under the TRIPS Agreement is that members must give effect to the provisions of the Agreement and accord the treatment provided for in the Agreement to the nationals of other members. A 'national' is understood as meaning those natural or legal persons who would be eligible for protection if all members of WTO were also bound by the Paris, Berne and Rome Conventions and by the Washington Treaty on Intellectual Property in Respect of Integrated Circuits (the 'IPIC Treaty').

Members are free to determine the appropriate method of implementing the provisions of the TRIPS Agreement within their own legal system and practice, and may implement more extensive protection than is required, provided that such additional protection does not contravene other provisions of the Agreement (Articles 1.1 and 1.3).

2.1.4 World Intellectual Property Organization Copyright Treaty (1996)

At the World Intellectual Property Organization (WIPO) diplomatic conference in December 1996 proposals for three new copyright treaties were received and discussed. The treaties were drafted jointly by the European Commission and the USA. The treaties concerned:

- Copyright (WIPO Copyright Treaty, WCT)
- Performers and producers of phonograms (WIPO Performances and Phonograms Treaty, WPPT)
- Protection of databases (this one was deferred).

The WCT and the WPPT included:

- a definition of the reproduction right to include all temporary and incidental copies
- a communication to the public right to prohibit unauthorized transmission by any telecommunication method
- legal protection against circumvention for digital rights management systems.

The WCT was concluded in 1996 and has 93 contracting parties. The WCT entered into force on 6 March 2002. It was introduced to adapt the global copyright regime to the challenges posed by the advent of the digital world, notably the internet. The WCT mentions two categories of copyright works, namely computer programs and compilations of data or other material. The WCT also deals with three exclusive rights:

1 distribution right
2 rental right
3 right of communication to the public.

2.1.5 Marrakesh Treaty (2013)

The Marrakesh Treaty to facilitate access to published works for persons who are blind, visually impaired or otherwise print-disabled (www.wipo.int/treaties/en/ip/marrakesh) was adopted in 2013. It is administered by WIPO, but at the time of writing the Treaty was not yet in force.

The main goal of the Marrakesh Treaty is to create a set of mandatory limitations and exceptions for the benefit of the blind, visually impaired and otherwise print-disabled. It requires contracting parties to introduce a standard set of copyright exceptions to allow for the reproduction, distribution and making available of published works in formats that are accessible to visually impaired persons (VIPs). It goes further than the current disability exceptions in the CDPA 1988 (which can be found at ss 31A, 31B and 31BA) because it crucially permits the exchange of these works across borders by organizations that serve VIPs.

Only works that are 'in the form of text, notation and/or related illustrations, whether published or otherwise made available in any media' fall within the scope of the Treaty, and that does include audiobooks.

A crucial aspect of the Treaty is the 'authorized entities' that are able to perform cross-border exchanges. Cross-border transfer by authorized entities is not permitted unless the contracting party in which the copy is made is a party to the WIPO Copyright Treaty or otherwise applies the three-step test. The definition of authorized entities encompasses many not-for-profit and government entities that are either specifically authorized or are recognized by the government as entities which provide educational functions and information access to VIPs. These authorized entities have a number of duties and responsibilities laid upon them (see Article 2 of the Marrakesh Treaty):

- to establish that the people they serve are beneficiary persons
- to distribute and make available accessible format copies only to those beneficiaries
- to discourage the reproduction, distribution and making available of unauthorized copies
- to maintain 'due care' in the handling of copies of works.

Authorized entities may, on a non-profit basis, make copies in accessible formats, which can be distributed by non-commercial lending or by electronic communication; the conditions for this activity include having lawful access to the work, introducing only those changes needed to make the work accessible, and supplying the copies only for use by beneficiary persons. VIPs may also make a personal use copy where they have lawful access to a copy of a work. At the domestic level countries can confine limitations or exceptions to those works that cannot be 'obtained commercially under reasonable terms for beneficiary persons in that market'. Use of this possibility requires notification to the WIPO Director General.

The UK is one of the 82 signatories to the Treaty, although at the time of writing there were only eight accessions/ratifications, and the UK wasn't one of the countries that had ratified the treaty. It requires the deposit of 20 instruments of ratification or accession by eligible parties in order for the Treaty to come into force.

2.1.6   Treaty Proposal on Copyright Limitations and Exceptions for Libraries and Archives

The Treaty Proposal on Copyright Limitations and Exceptions for Libraries and Archives (known by the acronym TLIB) is a draft WIPO treaty. It is important for libraries and archives because if the treaty were to be passed it would ensure that participating countries implemented a number of exceptions. It is important for the work of libraries in areas such as preservation, document supply and inter-library loan, as well as the lending of digital works. Having in place the proposed treaty on exceptions and limitations would, for example, ensure that libraries were able to undertake cross-border inter-library loans.

Articles 5–14 of TLIB deal with a number of mandatory exceptions:

- right to parallel importation
- right to acquire works
- right to library and archive lending and temporary access
- right to reproduction and supply of copies by libraries and archives
- right of preservation of library and archival materials
- right to use works and material protected by related rights for the benefit of persons with disabilities
- right to access retracted and withdrawn works
- right to use of orphan works and materials protected by related rights
- right to cross-border uses
- right to translate works and materials by libraries and archives.

2.1.7   Sources of information on international copyright laws

Figure 2.1 gives sources of further information on the copyright laws of other countries.

WIPO Lex www.wipo.int/wipolex/en ★
Collection of national copyright laws (UNESCO)
www.unesco.org/culture/copyrightlaws
The EU copyright legal framework ('acquis') http://ec.europa.eu/internal_market/
copyright/acquis/index_en.htm

Figure 2.1 *Sources for finding the copyright laws of other countries*

2.2 European legislation

Changes to UK copyright law are often the result of developments at a European level. The aim of the European Commission is to harmonize copyright laws in the member states in order to achieve a level playing field for copyright protection across national borders so that the Single Market can become a reality for new products and services containing intellectual property.

EU laws become part of UK law by virtue of the European Communities Act 1972. EU laws take precedence over existing UK laws which, if they are found to be in conflict with EU law, must be amended.

The European Union is founded on a number of treaties. The EU has three types of legislative acts, and these are regulations, directives and decisions.

- **Regulations** have general application. They are binding in their entirety and are directly applicable in all member states.
- **Directives** are binding on each member state to which they are addressed in terms of the end results to be achieved. But unlike regulations, it is left to the national authorities to make the choice of form and methods by which the results are achieved.
- **Decisions** are binding in their entirety on those to whom they are addressed.

There is another form of documentation, namely **Opinions and recommendations**, although these have no binding force.

The vast majority of EU legislation is enacted in the UK by statutory instrument under section 2(2) of the European Communities Act 1972, although some pieces of EU legislation are enacted through Acts of Parliament. These are a couple of examples:

- The Data Protection Act 1998 implements Directive 95/46/EC on the protection of individuals with regard to the processing of personal data and on the free movement of such data
- The Copyright and Rights in Performances (Certain Permitted Uses of Orphan Works) Regulations 2014 implement Directive 2012/28/EU on certain permitted uses of orphan works.

There is a **website for monitoring the progress of European legislation**, the
✱ European Parliament's legislative observatory, www.europarl.europa.eu/oeil/
home/home.do.

The Official Journal is the official compendium of all EU legal acts. The Official
Journal is split into three parts (see Table 2.1). The EUR-Lex website, http://eur-lex.
europa.eu/homepage.html, gives access to the Official Journals and their content.

Table 2.1 *Official Journal of the European Union*	
OJ C series	Resolutions, recommendations and opinions Information Preparatory acts Notices Announcements
OJ L series	Legislative acts Non-legislative acts (including decisions, recommendations, guidelines, rules of procedure)
OJ S series	Public contracts and tenders

2.2.1   European regulations

There are a number of European regulations relevant to intellectual property
rights. They include:

- Regulation 864/2007 on the law applicable to non-contractual obligations
  (Rome II). This establishes that the law applicable to a non-contractual
  obligation resulting from the infringement of an intellectual property right is
  that of the country for which the protection was sought and that there can be
  no derogation to this provision (see Article 8 of the regulation on the
  infringement of intellectual property rights).
- Regulation 386/2012 on entrusting the Office for Harmonization in the
  Internal Market with tasks related to the enforcement of intellectual property
  rights. The regulation makes OHIM fully responsible for the European
  Observatory on Infringements of Intellectual Property Rights
  https://oami.europa.eu/ohimportal/en/web/observatory/home.
- Council regulation 608/2013 concerning customs enforcement of intellectual
  property rights and repealing council regulation 1383/2003. The purpose of the
  regulation is to strengthen the enforcement of intellectual property rights in the
  light of the increase in counterfeit and pirated goods entering into the EU and it
  can in certain specific circumstances apply to counterfeit or pirated goods in
  transit.

2.2.2   European directives

There have been a number of European directives on copyright over the past two
decades. These are summarized in Table 2.2.

Table 2.2 *Summary of European directives on copyright*

Directive number	Title	Implemented in the UK by
2009/24/EC	On the legal protection of computer programs	SI 1992/3233
2006/115/EC	On the rental and lending right and certain related rights	SI 1996/2967
93/83/EEC	On the co-ordination of certain rules concerning copyright and rights related to copyright applicable to satellite broadcasting and cable retransmission	SI 1996/2967
2006/116/EC	Harmonizing the term of protection of copyright and certain related rights	SI 1995/3297
96/9/EC	On the legal protection of databases	SI 1997/3032, amended by SI 2003/2501
2001/29/EC	On the harmonization of certain aspects of copyright and related rights in the information society	SI 2003/2498
2001/84/EC	On the resale right for the benefit of the author of an original work of art	SI 2006/346 as amended by SI 2009/2792 and SI 2011/2873
2004/48/EC	On the enforcement of intellectual property rights	SI 2006/1028
2011/77/EU	Amending Directive 2006/116/EC on the term of protection of copyright and certain related rights	SI 2013/1782 (see also the amending SI 2014/434)
2012/28/EU	On certain permitted uses of orphan works	SI 2014/2861
2014/26/EU	On collective management of copyright and related rights and multi-territorial licensing of rights in musical works for online use in the internal market	(Implementation is required by 10 April 2016)

2.2.2.1 Directive 2009/24/EC on the legal protection of computer programs (replaces 91/250/EEC)

The aim of the directive is to harmonize the member states' legislation regarding the protection of computer programs in order to prevent the unauthorized reproduction of software. Computer programs are protected as literary works, which gives them the full protection of the Berne Convention. The term 'computer program' includes preparatory design work leading to the development of a program, provided that the nature of the preparatory work is such that a computer program can result from it at a later stage.

2.2.2.2   Directive 2006/115/EC on rental and lending right (replaces 92/100/EEC)

Authors and performers have an exclusive right to authorize or prohibit rental and lending of their works. 'Rental' means making available for use for a limited period of time and for direct or indirect economic or commercial advantage. 'Lending' means making available for use for a limited period of time and not for direct or indirect economic or commercial advantage. The directive provides for a harmonization of the rights of fixation, reproduction, broadcasting and communication to the public and distribution. The directive addresses collective management as a model for the management of the equitable remuneration right, but does not make it a requirement. So long as authors obtain remuneration for the lending of their works, member states are able to derogate from the exclusive public lending right. Member states are prevented from applying international exhaustion of the distribution right.

2.2.2.3   Directive 93/83/EEC on the co-ordination of certain rules concerning copyright and rights related to copyright applicable to satellite broadcasting and cable retransmission

The directive aims to facilitate the cross-border transmission of audiovisual programmes, notably broadcasting via satellite and retransmission by cable. With this in mind, it sets up mechanisms to ensure that creators and producers of programmes obtain a fair remuneration for the use of their creations.

2.2.2.4   Directive 2006/116/EC on harmonizing the term of copyright protection (replaces 93/98/EEC)

This directive harmonized the term of protection of copyright and neighbouring rights. It extended the term of protection for copyright literary, dramatic, musical and artistic works and films from 50 to 70 years after the year of the death of the author; and article 4 of the directive gave a new right – publication right – to works in which copyright had expired and which had not previously been published.

2.2.2.5   Directive 96/9/EC on the legal protection of databases

This introduced a new form of *sui generis* property protection for database producers valid for 15 years to prevent unfair extraction and re-utilization of the database contents. It did so in order to protect the investment of time, money and effort that goes into the selection and arrangement of the contents of databases, and where database right applies it does so regardless of whether or not the database could be considered to be innovative.

2.2.2.6   Directive 2001/29/EC on the harmonization of certain aspects of copyright and related rights in the information society

This directive, which is sometimes referred to as the 'Copyright Directive' or the 'InfoSoc Directive' is arguably the most important of all of the EU directives on copyright matters which have been passed. It enabled the EU and its member states to ratify the provisions of the two 1996 WIPO treaties – the WIPO Copyright Treaty and the WIPO Performers and Producers of Phonograms Treaty – and it also updated the law to incorporate new technology, including internet practices.

2.2.2.7   Directive 2001/84/EC on the resale right for the benefit of the author of an original work of art (droit de suite)

This provided an artist with a right to receive a royalty based on the price obtained for any resale of an original work of art, subsequent to the first transfer by the artist. The right does not apply, however, to resales which take place between private individuals without the participation of an art market professional. In those cases no royalty would be payable.

Resale of a work of art incurs a royalty of between 0.25% and 4% depending upon the sale price. However, the total amount of resale royalty payable on the sale must not in any event exceed €12,500. The directive has been implemented in the UK through The Artist's Resale Right Regulations 2006 SI 2006/346 and came into force for living artists on 1 January 2006. The Artist's Resale Right (Amendment) Regulations 2009 SI 2009/2792 delayed until January 2012 the application of the 2006 Regulations to the estates of deceased artists in the UK. There was a further set of amending regulations (SI 2011/2873) which were needed to ensure that the UK implementation is fully compliant with the Directive.

2.2.2.8   Directive 2004/48/EC on the enforcement of intellectual property rights

This requires all member states to apply effective, dissuasive and proportionate remedies and penalties against those engaged in counterfeiting and piracy and to create a level playing field for rights holders in the EU.

2.2.2.9   Directive 2011/77/EU amending Directive 2006/116/EC on the term of protection of copyright and certain related rights

The directive extends the term of protection of the rights of performers and phonogram producers on music recordings within the EU from 50 to 70 years. The directive requires the introduction of 'use it or lose it' clauses in the contracts linking performers to their record companies. This enables performers to get their rights back if the record producer doesn't market the sound recording during the extended period of protection. It also harmonizes the method of calculating the term of protection of songs and other musical compositions with words created by several authors. The term of protection will expire 70 years after the death of the last person to survive: the author of the lyrics or the composer of the music.

2.2.2.10   Directive 2012/28/EU on certain permitted uses of orphan works

The directive sets out common rules on the digitization and online display of orphan works by which it means works such as books, newspaper and magazine articles and films that are still protected by copyright but whose authors or other rights holders are not known or cannot be located or contacted to obtain copyright permissions. Orphan works form a significant part of the collections held by European libraries and their research value to academics and researchers wouldn't be fully realized without common rules to make their digitization and online display legally possible.

The directive requires member states to put in place measures that would permit the digitization and making available of orphan works by cultural institutions where they have been unable to locate the copyright owners even after having conducted a diligent search. The directive requires the introduction of an exception or limitation to cover the copying of orphan works. The details of the diligent searches are to be recorded in a publicly accessible online database managed by the OHIM. Where a work has been identified as orphan in one member state, there is mutual recognition of the orphan status across all member states.

The directive was implemented in the UK through SI 2014/2861 The Copyright and Rights in Performances (Certain Permitted Uses of Orphan Works) Regulations 2014.

2.2.2.11   Directive 2014/26/EU on collective management of copyright and related rights and multi-territorial licensing of rights in musical works for online use in the internal market

The directive sets out requirements necessary to ensure the proper functioning of the management of copyright and related rights by collective management organizations. It also lays down requirements for multi-territorial licensing by collective management organizations (CMOs) of authors' rights in musical works for online use.

The directive requires that member states regulate the operation of organizations which manage copyrights collectively on behalf of authors and rights holders. It addresses the governance of these organizations with obligations on societies with regard to issues such as annual meetings, collection and use of rights revenue, as well as ensuring that deductions for management fees can be properly justified. Under the directive, collecting societies are required to operate in the best interests of their members. The UK government needs to implement the directive by 10 April 2016.

2.3   UK legislation

The main piece of UK legislation governing copyright is the Copyright, Designs and Patents Act 1988. The Act has been amended by a number of other Acts of Parliament (such as the Copyright, etc. and Trade Marks (Offences and Enforcement) Act 2002, the Legal Deposit Libraries Act 2003, and the Enterprise and Regulatory Reform Act 2013) and by many statutory instruments over the course of the decades that have elapsed since the coming into force of the CDPA 1988.

It is important to ensure that when you look up the wording of legislation that an annotated copy of the legislation is used which fully incorporates any amendments that there may have been (which could, for example, include entire Acts or sections of Acts being repealed, amendments to the wording of sections which are in force, or where statutory instruments may have been revoked). This is especially true of the Copyright, Designs and Patents Act 1988 given the sheer volume of amending legislation which has been passed in the period since the original Act came into force.

A useful free resource for looking up UK legislation is www.legislation.gov.uk. ✷ The website is managed by The National Archives on behalf of the government. It incorporates amendments to Acts of Parliament, although not to statutory instruments. If you were to look at an SI on legislation.gov.uk it would merely inform you that 'This is the original version (as it was originally made). This item of legislation is currently only available in its original format.'

Fully annotated copies of legislation are available on commercial services such as Lexis and Westlaw. It is worth bearing in mind that there are limitations to relying on free resources. For example, even though Acts of Parliament are annotated on legislation.gov.uk, users of the site are regularly likely to find notices to the effect that: 'There are outstanding changes not yet made by the legislation.gov.uk editorial team to xyz Act. Those changes will be listed when you open the content using the Table of Contents.'

When using the website, in addition to being able to download a copy of the piece of legislation you are looking up, it is worth checking to see what supporting documentation there is. Using the example of The Copyright and Rights in Performances (Personal Copies for Private Use) Regulations 2014 (SI 2014/2361), in addition to the full text of the statutory instrument the legislation.gov.uk site also has a number of additional tabs which provide access to:

- explanatory memorandum
- impact assessment
- more resources – transposition note.

All content on the legislation.gov.uk website is available under the Open Government Licence v3.0, except where otherwise stated.

To illustrate the parliamentary progress of a bill through to its becoming an Act of Parliament, I will use the example of the Intellectual Property Act 2014. This started as a bill in the House of Lords. Its progress is charted in Table 2.3.

Table 2.3 Parliamentary progress of the Intellectual Property Bill through to Royal Assent		
1st reading	House of Lords	9 May 2013
2nd reading	House of Lords	22 May 2013
Committee stage: 1st sitting	House of Lords	11 June 2013
Committee stage: 2nd sitting	House of Lords	13 June 2013
Committee stage: 3rd sitting	House of Lords	18 June 2013
Report stage	House of Lords	23 July 2014
3rd reading	House of Lords	30 July 2014
1st reading	House of Commons	29 August 2013
2nd reading	House of Commons	20 January 2014
Programme motion	House of Commons	20 January 2014
Committee debate: 1st sitting	House of Commons	28 January 2014
Committee debate: 2nd sitting	House of Commons	28 January 2014
Committee debate: 3rd sitting	House of Commons	30 January 2014
Committee debate: 4th sitting	House of Commons	30 January 2014
Report stage	House of Commons	12 March 2014
3rd reading	House of Commons	12 March 2014
Ping pong	House of Lords	2 April 2014
Royal assent		14 May 2014

At the time of writing four commencement orders had been published, as well as a set of amending regulations:

- The Intellectual Property Act 2014 (Commencement No 1) Order 2014 SI 2014/1715
- The Intellectual Property Act 2014 (Commencement No 2) Order 2014 SI 2014/2069
- The Intellectual Property Act 2014 (Commencement No 3 and Transitional Provisions) Order 2014 SI 2014/2330
- The Intellectual Property Act 2014 (Commencement No 4) Order 2015: SI 2015/165
- The Intellectual Property Act 2014 (Amendment) Regulations 2014 SI 2014/2329.

The amending regulations were required to correct errors in the wording of the Act.

The website of the UK parliament (http://services.parliament.uk/bills) lists ✹ details of bills currently before parliament and which stages they have been through so far, along with versions of the bill, explanatory notes and amendments.

2.4   Case law

There are always grey areas of interpretation or circumstances where the law is unclear, and this is where case law comes in. Case law helps us understand how the legislation is to be applied in practice. Case law is important in England because of its common law heritage. It isn't sufficient merely to know what the legislation says. It is also important to be aware of any relevant case law which helps to shed light on how the legislation should be interpreted in practice, and especially where this is from the Court of Justice of the European Union or from the UK's Supreme Court.

When a UK judge makes a decision on a matter of law, he or she is required to follow the decisions of their predecessors and superiors. The hierarchy of the court system (see Figure 2.2) is important here because judgments are binding on all subsequent cases heard in courts at the same level or at a lower level in the hierarchy. Previous cases are therefore known as precedents.

A good example of a case which went through the various stages of the court hierarchy is the Meltwater case (PRCA v NLA C-360/13, [2013] UKSC 18; NLA v Meltwater Holding [2011]EWCA Civ 890, [2010] EWHC 3099 (Ch))(see Figure 2.3).

In the Meltwater case there were two entirely separate actions, one through the Copyright Tribunal and one through the High Court and beyond.

Meltwater, in conjunction with the Public Relations Consultants Association

```
Supreme Court      →    ┌──────────────┐
 ☐                      │ European     │
 ↑                 ←    │ Court of     │
 ☐                      │ Justice      │
Court of Appeal    →    │              │
 ☐                      │              │
                   ←    │              │
 ↑                      │              │
 ☐                      │              │
High Court         →    │              │
 ☐                      │              │
                   ←    │              │
 ↑                      │              │
 ☐                      │              │
County courts           └──────────────┘
```

Figure 2.2
The hierarchy of the civil courts in the UK

```
Supreme Court [2013] UKSC 18 (17 April 2013) →        European Court of Justice
                                                      [2014] CJEU
                                              ←       C-360/13 (5 June 2014)
 ↑                                                    ☐☐
Court of Appeal [2011] EWCA (Civ 890) (27 July 2011)
 ↑
High Court [2010] EWHC 3099 (Ch) (26 November 2010)
```

Figure 2.3 *Progress of the Meltwater case through the courts*

(the PRCA), referred the Newspaper Licensing Agency's (NLA) web licences for media monitoring agencies and their clients to the Copyright Tribunal. The Tribunal can only rule on the reasonableness of the terms of the licence, so their focus is on the commercial aspects of the licence. The Copyright Tribunal case reference is CT114/09, and the following decisions were published between 2010 and 2012: Decision and order 18 Mar 2010; Interim decision 14 Feb 2012; and Final decision 15 May 2012.

The NLA initiated a High Court action to clarify the legal aspect, notably their right to issue licences for aggregators and end-users. This was a landmark case which examined the s 28A exception on the making of temporary or transient copies, and the case ultimately went to the European Court of Justice (CJEU), which held that on-screen and cached copies of websites generated by users while they browse the web do not infringe the copyright of publishers. Had the Court decided otherwise, it would have meant that users could potentially infringe copyright merely by browsing publicly accessible websites (such as those of newspaper publishers). The CJEU judgment means that merely opening and reading a web page falls within the exception for the making of temporary or transient copies. (For a write-up of the case see Section 3.6.4.)

2.5   Sources of information on EU and UK legislation and case law

Figure 2.4 provides a summary of information sources.

UK legislation
www.legislation.gov.uk
www.parliament.uk
http://services.parliament.uk/bills/
EU legislation
http://ec.europa.eu/internal_market/copyright/acquis/index_en.htm
http://eur-lex.europa.eu/oj/direct-access.html
UK case law
www.bailii.org
EU case law
http://ipcuria.eu
http://curia.europa.eu

Figure 2.4
Sources of information on EU and UK legislation and case law

A free web resource covering UK case law is the website of the British & Irish Legal Information Institute, www.bailii.org. The site contains British and Irish case law and legislation, as well as European Union case law.

For European case law, there is a site called IP Curia.eu (http://ipcuria.eu), which contains CJEU case law on intellectual property. It only covers decisions from the CJEU which are published in English and which relate to intellectual property law. The site lists recent decisions and appeals. The database has a full text search facility, and it is also possible to browse the case law by the relevant directive, and the relevant article that the case relates to (for example, it can be used to locate which cases look at the interpretation of Directive 2001/29/EC, and specifically at article 3, on the right of communication to the public).

The way in which the English common law system works means that English laws are made up of both legislation and case law. Legal precedent is made by judges sitting in court. It is important to look at not only the wording of the primary legislation in the form of Acts of Parliament and the secondary legislation in the form of statutory instruments in order to understand what the law on copyright is, but also at the constantly developing and changing body of case law which has built up over many years, because this helps to interpret, clarify and understand how the legislation applies in specific cases by applying the unique facts of a particular case to the codified law.

Notes

1   http://ec.europa.eu/internal_market/copyright/acquis/index_en.htm.
2   There are also recommendations and opinions which it is not mandatory to follow.

CHAPTER 3

Acts permitted in relation to copyright works (The Copyright Exceptions)

3.1   Introduction

Copyright law gives to the author as the first owner a number of exclusive rights, as set out in section 16 of the CDPA 1988. These are the right:

- to copy the work
- to issue copies of the work to the public
- to rent or lend the work to the public
- to perform, show or play the work in public
- to communicate the work to the public
- to make an adaptation of the work or do any of the above in relation to an adaptation.

To do any of the above acts without the permission of the rights holder would be a primary infringement of copyright. However, the Berne Convention of 1886 does allow national governments to implement exceptions to these exclusive rights provided that the exceptions meet three criteria. This is known as the Berne three-step test. Works can be reproduced:

> in certain special cases, provided that such reproduction does not conflict with a normal exploitation of the work and does not unreasonably prejudice the legitimate interests of the author.[1]

The Copyright Directive (2001/29/EC) is intended to harmonize certain aspects of copyright and related rights in the information society. Article 5 of that directive covers Exceptions and Limitations, and Article 5(5) contains substantially the same form of words as the Berne Convention's three-step test. As a result, the UK's copyright legislation must only contain copyright exceptions or permitted acts which meet all of the criteria specified in the three-step test.

In the directive there is one compulsory exception on the making of temporary copies (see Section 3.6.4), and this is then followed by an exhaustive list of other exceptions which are available to the EU member countries to pick and choose from. As a result the exceptions and limitations aren't truly harmonized across the European Union.

The majority of the available exceptions can be found in Article 5 of the Copyright Directive (2001/29/EC). Other exceptions can be found in the Software Directive (2009/24/EC) and the Database Directive (96/9/EEC). In addition a more recent exception can be found in the Orphan Works Directive (2012/28/EU). Article 6 of The Orphan Works Directive (2012/28/EU) says that:

> Member States shall provide for an exception or limitation to the right of reproduction and the right of making available to the public provided for respectively in Articles 2 and 3 of Directive 2001/29/EC to ensure that the organizations referred to in Article 1(1) are permitted to use orphan works contained in their collections in the following ways:
>
> (a) by making the orphan work available to the public, within the meaning of Article 3 of Directive 2001/29/EC;
> (b) by acts of reproduction, within the meaning of Article 2 of Directive 2001/29/EC, for the purposes of digitization, making available, indexing, cataloguing, preservation or restoration.
>
> Source: Article 6, Directive 2012/28/EU

The UK's copyright exceptions are set out in the CDPA 1988 Chapter III: 'Acts permitted in relation to copyright works'. Librarians and information professionals should ensure that they consult an up-to-date annotated copy of the Act. The copyright exceptions underwent a major overhaul during the course of 2014, and it is essential that librarians are relying on the correct wording of the law as amended.

Even if there is a copyright exception which you think that you might be able to rely on (and when I use the word 'you' I am referring here both to library and information professionals copying on behalf of their users, and also to researchers wishing to copy material themselves) there are a number of points to consider:

- Is the amount that can be copied under the exception limited by fair dealing?
- Does the exception incorporate a clause preventing contracts from overriding the exception?
- Is the exception only available for a non-commercial purpose?
- Is the exception only available for use by not-for-profit publicly accessible libraries, the libraries of educational establishments, museums or galleries?
- Is there anything else which places restrictions on those wishing to use the exception, for example:

— the copy must have been lawfully acquired
— the person copying must have lawful access to the work
— where it is not reasonably practical to purchase a replacement copy?

One point of contention amongst the user community and their representatives has been the interrelationship between contract and copyright. Before the changes to the copyright exceptions which implemented the recommendations of the *Hargreaves Review* took effect in 2014, contract law could be used to override almost all of the exceptions, thereby rendering them worthless. The *Hargreaves Review* says:

> Even where there are copyright exceptions established by law, administrators are often forced to prevent staff and students exercising them, because of restrictive contracts.[2]

To address this problem, Hargreaves makes clear that:

> the government should also legislate to ensure that (these and other) copyright exceptions are protected from override by contract.

Following the implementation of the recommendations made in the *Hargreaves Review*, quite a few of the copyright exceptions now include clauses which prevent contract override. It is important, however, to bear in mind that there isn't a general provision preventing all of the exceptions from being overridden by contract. Instead, anybody who intends to rely on a particular copyright exception needs to look at the exception wording to see whether it incorporates a form of words preventing contract override. A typical form of words to look out for is:

> To the extent that a term of a contract purports to prevent or restrict the doing of any act which, by virtue of this section, would not infringe copyright, that term is unenforceable.

In other words, even if the wording of a contract were to try and take away the ability to use the exception in question, that clause would be deemed to be invalid and as such it would therefore be unenforceable.

Table 3.1 on the next page lists copyright exceptions which cannot be overridden by contracts and Table 3.2 explores the interface between copyright exceptions and licences.

With a licence like the ones available from the Copyright Licensing Agency (CLA) there will be some titles that cannot be copied under the CLA licence; and where that applies you could then consider whether one of the exceptions would cover the particular instance of copying that you want to do. However, you would need to bear in mind that the copyright exceptions are narrow in scope, and you would therefore have to ensure that your instance of copying fell within the scope of the exception and any conditions that qualified its use.

Table 3.1 *Copyright exceptions that cannot be overridden by contracts*

Section number in the CDPA 1988	Exception
s 29	Research and private study
s 29A	Copies for text and data analysis for non-commercial research
s 30(1ZA)	Quotation
s 30A	Caricature, parody or pastiche
s 31A	Disabled persons: copies of works for personal use
s 31B	Making and supply of accessible copies (for disabled persons) by authorized bodies
s 31BA	Making and supply of intermediate copies (for disabled persons) by authorized bodies
s 32	Illustration for instruction
s 41	Copying by librarians: supply of single copies to other libraries
s 42	Copying by librarians: replacement copies of works
s 42A	Copying by librarians: single copies of published works
s 50A	Back-up copies of computer programs
s 50B	Decompilation
s 50BA	Observing, studying and testing of computer programs
s 50D	Acts permitted in relation to databases
s 75	Recording of a broadcast for archival purposes
s 36(7)	Copying and use of extracts of works by educational establishments No contract can limit the amount that may be copied to being less than 5% of a work in any 12-month period

Table 3.2 *The interface between exceptions and licences*

Copyright exceptions	Licences
Acts of copying which are permitted through provisions set out in the law (Chapter III of the CDPA 1988 as amended) without the need to obtain a licence/permission from the copyright owner.	A licence gives permission to do something that, without there being a licence in place, would be an infringement of copyright. Based on contract law and industry practice, licences vary in scope and complexity. It could, for example, be a consent to use a photograph; a licence to allow a film to be based on a novel; an end-user licence for an e-book or a licence for a library to have access to a database of journals published by a specific publisher.
They are available free of charge.	They will often involve a cost, but not necessarily (for example the Creative Commons licences and the Open Government Licence don't involve a charge).

Table 3.2 *Continued*	
They will usually specify that proper acknowledgement should be given, unless this is impractical.	Even if the licence doesn't say anything about acknowledgement or giving proper credit, it is good practice to do so. A licence may well specify precisely what form the acknowledgement should take.
They will usually specify the purpose for which the exception can be used. In many cases that will be non-commercial.	If an exception is limited to non-commercial purposes, then a licence agreement may provide the solution to enable commercial use to be made of the work in exchange for a fee.
Some of the copyright exceptions are only available to the extent that there isn't a licensing scheme in place. Examples include: The exception for abstracts of scientific or technical articles in s 60 of the CDPA 1988 says that 'This section does not apply if or to the extent that there is a licensing scheme certified for the purposes of this section under section 143 providing for the grant of licences. The exception on recording by educational establishments of broadcasts in s 35 of the CDPA 1988 which says that 'Acts which would otherwise be permitted by this section are not permitted if, or to the extent that, licences are available authorizing the acts in question and the educational establishment responsible for those acts knew or ought to have been aware of that fact.'	In the case of abstracts (s 60), there isn't a licensing scheme in operation, and therefore the exception can be relied upon. In the case of broadcasts (s 35), where material is covered by a licensing scheme such as the one from the Educational Recording Agency (ERA), then the exception cannot be used.
	Where copyright licensing (or the lack of it) interferes with free markets, competition law and the use of compulsory licensing may be used to overcome issues of price fixing, price discrimination, or where the use of licensing is unfair.
Copyright exceptions can be overridden by licence agreements unless there is a provision clearly stating otherwise, such as 'To the extent that a term of a contract purports to prevent or restrict the doing of any act which, by virtue of this section, would not infringe copyright, that term is unenforceable.' A couple of examples of where contracts can override copyright exceptions are the exception on dedicated terminals (s 40B) and public administration (s 47).	The law doesn't allow changes to contractual agreements or licences which take place retrospectively. However, where a licence agreement was signed prior to a legislative change taking effect: If you have a licence granted before the new laws came into force, and it permits a wider range of activities than the new laws, then your licence will be unaffected. However, if the reverse is true – that the new laws allow you to do more than your licence, it means that while your licence is still valid, you can use the work under the exception without infringing copyright. Source: https://www.gov.uk/government/uploads/system/uploads/attachment_data/file/375951/Education_and-Teaching.pdf.

It would be misleading to suggest that the difference between exceptions and licences was simply based on which publication you were planning to copy, because it could well be that whilst a particular title can in theory be copied under an exception, your particular copying request would not qualify under the exception. For example:

- if the exception is subject to fair dealing, and if your use couldn't be said to be fair and reasonable
- if the exception were limited to copying for a non-commercial purpose, and if your use was for a commercial purpose.

When might you use a licence rather than rely on an exception?

- if the purpose of the copying is not covered by the exception
- if the extent of the copying goes beyond fair dealing (for example, if it involved multiple copies of a substantial part of the work).

★ Guidance on the copyright exceptions is available on the Intellectual Property Office website at www.gov.uk/exceptions-to-copyright.

3.2   Fair dealing

The phrase 'fair dealing' is a legal term which is used in order to establish whether a use of material protected by copyright is lawful, or whether it infringes copyright. The problem is that there is no statutory definition of what the term means. Instead, if anyone were to try and determine whether or not a particular act of copying was fair they would have to consider the specific factors involved in that particular instance of copying. The courts decide what is fair on a case-by-case basis. Only a few fair dealing copyright cases are decided in the courts each year.

It will always be a matter of fact, degree and impression in each specific case as to whether or not a particular act of copying was fair dealing. The key question to ask is 'what would a fair-minded and honest person think?' Given the circumstances involved, how would they have dealt with the work? There are several factors which have been identified by the courts as being relevant when determining whether a particular instance of copying of a work is fair or not. These factors include:

1 Does the way in which the work has been used affect the market for the original work? Does it harm the rights holder's ability to market or sell the work? If the use of the work can be said to act as a substitute for the original work and thereby lead to the rights holder losing money, it is unlikely that it would be considered to be fair.

2 A second factor relates to the amount of the work that has been taken. Is the

amount that has been used reasonable and appropriate? Was it strictly necessary to use that amount? Normally 'fair dealing' would only permit the copying of a part of a work.

Insubstantial amounts are never an infringement, but when referring to amount one needs to take account of the amount that has been copied both in terms of quantity as well as in qualitative terms. Is it the most useful, the most valuable, part of the work that has been copied? The term 'substantial part' is not defined in copyright law. It isn't just a question of quantity, but also of quality. The phrase has been interpreted by the courts to mean a qualitatively significant part of a work even where this is not a large part of the work in terms of quantity. As a result it is extremely difficult to decide whether or not something would constitute a substantial part. It is perfectly possible for a small portion of a work to constitute a substantial part (for examples of what courts have considered to be substantial parts of various different works see Figure 7.2, p. 151). The relative importance of any one factor will vary according to the case in hand and the type of dealing in question.

A fair dealing copy of a work must be accompanied by a sufficient acknowledgement, such as in a reference or bibliography. There is a definition in section 178 of the CDPA 1988 of what constitutes a sufficient acknowledgement:

'sufficient acknowledgement' means an acknowledgement identifying the work in question by its title or other description, and identifying the author unless –

(a) in the case of a published work, it is published anonymously;
(b) in the case of an unpublished work, it is not possible for a person to ascertain the identity of the author by reasonable inquiry

Source: The National Archives, 2015

The fair dealing exceptions normally state something to the effect that no acknowledgement is required where this would be impossible for reasons of practicality or otherwise.

3.2.1   Research (s 29)

Copyright law permits reasonable copying of all types of copyright works for non-commercial research and private study, without permission from the copyright holder. For example, researchers and students who need to copy parts of sound recordings, films or broadcasts for non-commercial research or private study are allowed to do so. However, they cannot use the exception as a general justification for copying any film they wish to watch. The exception only permits copying of what is strictly necessary for genuine non-commercial research or private study, so the film would have to be genuinely relevant to their course, or to some other independent study.

Companies are highly unlikely to be able to access material for free when they do research, because the exception only applies to non-commercial research. Anyone carrying out commercial research will have to obtain works under a licence.

The copying must be both fair and reasonable. In other words, the amount that can be copied is limited to fair dealing. Therefore, this rules out unfair or unreasonable uses such as copying a whole film for 'research' instead of buying the DVD. Copying a whole work would not generally be 'fair dealing'. In order to make a complete copy the researcher will need a licence to do so or to purchase a copy of the work. The fair dealing provisions generally mean that only a part of a work can be copied.

The law does not require copies made under the research or private study exception to be deleted once the research project is over, but where a person has made copies for the purposes of non-commercial research or private study they would not be permitted to use those copies for a commercial purpose at a later date.

3.2.2   Commercial v. non-commercial purpose

The UK Intellectual Property Office (IPO) chose not to define within the legislation what constitutes copying for a commercial purpose. Indeed, even if they were to do so, they would be second-guessing the European Court of Justice, which has the final say on the matter. The IPO took the view that if they were to try to define it, it would be likely to result in less flexibility for libraries and researchers.

Where the copying is undertaken by librarians on behalf of their users under the library exceptions, the copyright declaration form requires the reader to say that the copying they have asked to have done is for a non-commercial research purpose or private study. The form of words which would appear on the form would be along the lines 'I will not use the copy except for research for a non-commercial purpose or private study and will not supply a copy of it to any other person'.

The distinction between commercial and non-commercial came about as a result of Directive 2001/29/EC on the harmonization of certain aspects of copyright and related rights in the information society which was implemented in the UK through SI 2003/2498. Recital 42 of the 2001 directive says:

> When applying the exception or limitation for non-commercial educational and scientific research purposes, including distance learning, the non-commercial nature of the activity in question should be determined by that activity as such. The organizational structure and the means of funding of the establishment concerned are not the decisive factors in this respect.

However, the implementation of the Database Directive (96/9/EEC) through SI

1997/3032 represents the first instance of UK legislation making a distinction between commercial and non-commercial purpose.

Figure 3.1 sums up the key points on defining 'commercial purpose'.

- The legislation doesn't define 'commercial purpose'.
- The European Court of Justice has the final say.
- The test is whether the research is for a commercial purpose, not whether it is done by a commercial body (see the wording of recital 42 of the Copyright Directive 2001/29/EC).
- You can only decide on whether the purpose is commercial based on the facts available at the time of the copying. You cannot be expected to be a fortune teller.
- Think of it as income-generating, not necessarily profit-making.
- Some research in a commercial environment could be classed as non-commercial.
- Some research in a non-commercial environment could be classed as commercial.
- The concept was explored in the case of HM Stationery Office v Green Amps Ltd [2007] EWHC 2755 (Ch).

Figure 3.1 *Key points about 'commercial purpose'*

3.2.3   Private study (s 29)

Section 178 of the CDPA 1988 on minor definitions makes clear that copying for the purposes of private study only covers non-commercial copying:

> 'private study' does not include any study which is directly or indirectly for a commercial purpose
>
> Source: The National Archives, 2015

In the case of both research and private study, there is a provision in section 29(3) which places restrictions on situations where the copying is done by someone other than the researcher or student themselves:

> 29(3) Copying by a person other than the researcher or student himself is not fair dealing if
>
> (a) in the case of a librarian, or a person acting on behalf of a librarian, that person does anything which is not permitted under section 42A (copying by librarians: single copies of published works), or
> (b) in any other case, the person doing the copying knows or has reason to believe that it will result in copies of substantially the same material being provided to more than one person at substantially the same time and for substantially the same purpose.
>
> Source: IPO, 2014

This is to prevent people from trying to obtain the whole or a substantial part of the work in this way, because that would not be considered to be fair dealing.

3.2.4   Illustration for instruction (s 32)

Section 32 of the CDPA 1988 permits fair dealing for the purpose of illustration for instruction. In the CDPA 1988 it appears as the first of the series of educational exceptions, and so the detail of this exception and how it works can be found in Section 3.4.1. However, while the exceptions in sections 33–36A are only intended for use by educational establishments, section 32 is different. The section 32 fair dealing exception applies to acts of teaching in general, and it is not restricted to teaching undertaken by educational establishments. It would, for example, cover other providers of instruction such as museums and youth organizations. (For more detail about this exception see Section 3.4.1 below, where it is considered within a section on the educational exceptions.)

3.2.5   Quotation (s 30)

The quotation exception permits people to quote from the works of others without the permission of the owner, as long as the use is proportionate and fair. It is worth noting that the exception covers the use of a quotation from a work whether it be for a commercial or a non-commercial purpose.

For example, the quotation of a title or short extract in an academic article may be considered fair, and be permitted under this exception, as would a short quotation that is necessary and relevant in an essay; whereas the copying of a long extract from a book, without it being justified by its context, would not be permitted.

Copyright law previously permitted the use of quotations or extracts, without requiring permission from copyright owners, if such use was 'fair' but this was limited to situations where it was being done for the purpose of criticism, review or reporting current events. The introduction of the section 30(1ZA) exception for quotation purposes means that other uses of extracts are now covered. So, for example, quotations for illustration or analysis such as a quotation consisting of a lyric or a few bars of music. The following conditions apply to the exception:

1 the work must have been made available to the public,
2 the use of the quotation must be fair dealing with the work,
3 the extent of the quotation must be no more than is required by the specific purpose for which it is used, and
4 the quotation must be accompanied by a sufficient acknowledgement (unless this would be impossible for reasons of practicality or otherwise).

The quotation exception came into force on 1 October 2014. UK copyright law had long allowed fair quotation of extracts from copyright works for the purpose of criticism or review, as long as there was a sufficient acknowledgement of the source of the quotation.

The Copyright and Rights in Performances (Quotation and Parody)

Regulations 2014 SI 2014/2356 broadened the provisions in s 30 by inserting s 30(1ZA) to permit quotation from a work not only for the purpose of criticism or review, but for any purpose, as long as it is a 'fair dealing' in the work. This allows other minor uses of quotations, such as academic citation and use in examination papers, which do not undermine the commercial exploitation of copyright works.

The quotation exception applies to all types of copyright work, including film, broadcasts, sound recordings and photographs, as well as traditional text quotations. Before the s 30(1ZA) exception came into force the previous law restricted freedom of expression by preventing free use of quotations, even where a quote was very short.

The quotation exception within section 30(1ZA) is in addition to, rather than a replacement for, the exception for criticism, review and news reporting.

The exception certainly does not mean that people can 'quote' any amount of copyright material for free. Rather, it only allows the use of material for the purpose of quotation to a fair extent. The legislation does not specify a limit to the number of words that can be copied under the quotation exception. The accompanying impact assessment does, however, provide more detailed information. It is noteworthy that the guidance given in the impact assessment changed significantly between the draft impact assessment and the final version which was published once the Regulations had been finalized.

Based on their own analysis of reference works the IPO estimate the average 'fair' quotation in a reference work of 500 words per page to be about 50 words long (1/10th of the page), and now speak of the average fair quotation in a reference work to be about 50 words long. The IPO say that fair dealing is a flexible concept and there may be some exceptional or rare instances where the copying of 400 words would be permitted. A quotation is less likely to be considered 'fair' the longer it is. The exception limits what can be copied for the purposes of quotation to situations where the length or extent of the quote(s) used is necessary and without it being so extensive that it would compete with sales of the original work, as this would remove the need for people to buy a copy of the work, thereby depriving the copyright owner of income.

The final impact assessment also cites a number of sets of guidelines, such as the STM guidelines for quotation and other academic uses.[3]

3.2.6   Criticism and review (s 30)

The section 30(1) exception covers copying for the purpose of criticism or review, so long as:

- the copying is fair dealing with the work
- a sufficient acknowledgement is made, unless this would be impossible for reasons of practicality or otherwise

- the work has been made available to the public. 'Made available to the public' means that the work has been made available by any means, including:
  — the issue of copies to the public
  — making the work available by means of an electronic retrieval system
  — the rental or lending of copies of the work to the public
  — the performance, exhibition, playing or showing of the work in public
  — the communication to the public of the work .

In order to fall within the criticism and review exception, it shouldn't simply involve duplicating long extracts from the work in question. Reviewers should only use what is needed for the purpose of doing the review of the work. So if you are the reviewer, it would be advisable to ask yourself whether you are really using the copyright work for the purposes of criticism, review and comment, or whether you are actually making use of the work for some other purpose, and are merely citing the criticism and review exception as the legal justification for your use of the work. In order to qualify for this exception, the review should evaluate the contents of the work.

The exception isn't limited to reviewing or criticizing the style or content of a particular work. Indeed, it could cover criticism of the ideas to be found in the work and their social or moral implications. In the case of Hubbard v Vosper [1972] 2 QB 84 it is clear that a literary work consists not just of the literary style but also of the thoughts which underlie it; and that under the criticism and review defence, both of those things can be criticized. So Mr Vosper was entitled to criticize not just the literary style, but also the doctrine or philosophy of Mr Hubbard as expounded in the books.

3.2.7   News reporting (s 30)

Section 30(2) says:

> Fair dealing with a work (other than a photograph) for the purpose of reporting current events does not infringe any copyright in the work provided that (subject to subsection (3)) it is accompanied by a sufficient acknowledgement
>
> Source: The National Archives, 2015

So the key points about the exception are:

- that it is subject to fair dealing
- it covers works apart from photographs
- it should be accompanied by a sufficient acknowledgement.

However, section 30(3) makes clear that no acknowledgement is required where the reporting of current events is done by means of a sound recording, film or broadcast where this would be impossible for reasons of practicality or otherwise.

A person would have a defence against a claim for copyright infringement if they could show that their use of the copyright material was fair dealing with the work for the purpose of reporting current events and if they had provided an adequate acknowledgement.

In Pro Sieben v Carlton [1998] EWCA Civ 2001 the use of a 30-second extract from a Carlton programme – an interview with Mandy Allwood – was judged not to be a fair dealing with the work. One sentence from the judgment says: ' "Criticism or review" and "reporting current events" are expressions of wide and indefinite scope. Any attempt to plot their precise boundaries is doomed to failure.'

It isn't possible to come up with a general rule of thumb that would work in virtually all cases. Every case will have its own unique set of facts, and the judgment in each case will be made in the light of the specific circumstances of that particular case. The Channel 4 Producers Handbook has a set of fair dealing guidelines (at www.channel4.com/producers-handbook/c4-guidelines/fair-dealing-guidelines) which illustrates how the exception works.

The exception is used in order to report *current* events, and the question of what would constitute a current event will depend on just how current the event is and also on whether it is something which is genuinely newsworthy, rather than the exception being used merely as a device to try and justify the use of the clip in question.

3.2.8   Caricature, parody and pastiche (s 30A)

Copyright law allows people to make some limited, reasonable use of creative content protected by copyright, for the purpose of caricature, parody or pastiche, without having to obtain the permission of the rights holder. It is worth noting that the exception covers both commercial and non-commercial uses.

The Copyright and Rights in Performances (Quotation and Parody) Regulations 2014 SI 2014/2356 inserted an exception for caricature, parody and pastiche into section 30A of the CDPA 1988. The exception permits use of someone else's copyright material for the purposes of caricature, parody or pastiche – but only if the use is fair and proportionate. The exception establishes a limited basis on which caricature, parody and pastiche may be practised, without disproportionate costs, uncertainty and legal risk. For example, the use of a few lines of song for a parody sketch is likely to be considered fair, whereas use of a whole song would not be and would continue to require a licence. Although it is not a requirement under Article 5(3)(k) of the InfoSoc (Copyright) Directive (2001/29/EC), the UK exception only permits use for the purposes of caricature, parody or pastiche to the extent that the use is 'fair dealing'.

Many works that are made for the purpose of caricature, parody or pastiche, especially in this age of digital creation and remixing, involve some level of copying from another work. Previously creators in the UK were liable for copyright infringement even if only a small amount of copying took place when a parody work was made. If the creator of the parody sought the permission of the owner of the rights in the work that they were parodying, it may have been granted in some cases, but there was no guarantee that permission would be granted. Indeed, it was often refused or else permission would have involved significant costs. Refusal to give permission could be said to impinge on an individual's freedom of expression, and the failure to secure relevant permissions ran the risk of legal action and potential damages.

It is important to bear in mind that creators still maintain their moral right to object to a derogatory treatment of their work (as set out in section 80 of the CDPA).

Key characteristics of the exception for caricature, parody or pastiche include the following:

- It is restricted to uses that are 'fair dealing' with the work – the use must be both fair and proportionate.
- The parody work must not be substitutable for the original work nor must it damage the commercial exploitation of the work.
- It covers uses for both commercial and for non-commercial purposes.

A CJEU case (Deckmyn v Vandersteen C-201/13) helps to clarify the way in which the exception works. It was established that the characteristics of a parody are as follows:

- It evokes an existing work.
- It is noticeably different from the existing work.
- It constitutes an expression of humour or mockery.
- A parody need not display an original character of its own, other than that of displaying noticeable differences with respect to the original work parodied.
- The application of the exception for parody established by Directive 2001/29/EC must strike a fair balance between, on the one hand, the interests and rights of authors and other rights holders and, on the other, the freedom of expression of the person who wishes to rely on that exception.
- If a parody conveys a discriminatory message, then the holder of the rights in the work that has been parodied does in principle have a legitimate interest in ensuring that their work is not associated with such a message.

3.3   Library exceptions

There are a group of exceptions in sections 40A–43A of the CDPA 1988 which are collectively known as the 'library exceptions'. They include exceptions for copying by librarians on behalf of their users; copying by librarians for other libraries; and copying by librarians for the purposes of conservation or replacement. Before examining the library exceptions in a bit more detail, it is worth looking at the list of library exceptions in order to get an overview of what they cover. The available exceptions are:

- s 40A, lending of copies by libraries or archives (see Section 3.3.2 below)
- s 40B, libraries and educational establishments, etc., making works available through dedicated terminals (see Section 3.3.3)
- s 41, copying by librarians: supply of single copies for other libraries (see Section 3.3.4)
- s 42, copying by librarians, etc.: replacement copies of works (see Section 3.3.5)
- s 42A, copying by librarians: single copies of published works (see Section 3.3.6)
- s 43, copying by librarians or archivists: single copies of unpublished works (see Section 3.3.7)
- s 43A, ss 40A to 43, interpretation (see Section 3.3.1).

3.3.1   Meaning of 'library' (s 43A)

In the past the library exceptions were for the benefit of 'prescribed libraries', and these were so called because Schedule 1 of The Copyright (Librarians and Archivists) (Copying of Copyright Material) Regulations 1989: SI 1989/1212 listed or 'prescribed' which types of library could benefit from the library exceptions.

The Copyright and Rights in Performances (Research, Education, Libraries and Archives) Regulations 2014: SI 2014/1372 introduced a number of changes to the library exceptions and one of these was to do away with the phrase 'prescribed library'. Instead the CDPA 1988 as amended refers to publicly accessible libraries, the libraries of educational establishments, museums and galleries. This is in keeping with the wording used in the Copyright Directive 2001/29/EC. The precise wording used in the CDPA 1988 is given here:

43A Sections 40A to 43: interpretation
(1) The following definitions have effect for the purposes of sections 40A to 43.
(2) "Library" means—
     (a) a library which is publicly accessible, or
     (b) a library of an educational establishment.
(3) "Museum" includes a gallery.

(4) "Conducted for profit", in relation to a library, archive or museum, means a body of that kind which is established or conducted for profit or which forms part of, or is administered by, a body established or conducted for profit.

(5) References to a librarian, archivist or curator include a person acting on behalf of a librarian, archivist or curator.

Source: The National Archives, 2015

This would seem to exclude some libraries which would previously have been covered as 'prescribed libraries', because of the requirement in the new wording that the libraries be 'publicly accessible'. The wording makes clear that 'library' means 'a library which is publicly accessible' or 'a library of an educational establishment'.

It follows logically from reading the wording in the Act as amended that publicly owned libraries that are not accessible to the public are not libraries for the purposes of making copies and are therefore debarred from making copies for preservation and replacement, making works available through dedicated terminals or indeed from benefiting from the other 'library exceptions'. But I am not a lawyer, and cannot give legal advice regarding how widely the phrase 'publicly accessible' should be interpreted.

The provisions relating to copying by librarians (etc.) on behalf of their users would cover a librarian, archivist, or curator of a library, archive or museum; and they would also cover a person acting on behalf of a librarian, archivist or curator.

What is clear is that the definition of a library entitled to benefit from the library exceptions only covers a library, archive, museum or gallery which is not conducted for profit and this means a body of a kind which is not established or conducted for profit or which forms part of, or is administered by, a body which is not established or conducted for profit.

3.3.2   Lending of copies by libraries or archives (s 40A)

Rental and lending of a work is a restricted act and as such, without section 40A being in place, it would require permission from the rights holder for public libraries to be able to lend books.

The distinction between rental and lending is that 'rental' means making a copy of the work available for use, on terms that it will or may be returned, for direct or indirect economic or commercial advantage; whereas 'lending' means making a copy of the work available for use, on terms that it will or may be returned, otherwise than for direct or indirect economic or commercial advantage.

Section 18A of the CDPA 1988 covers infringement by rental or lending of a work to the public. It is clear from s 18A that it is possible to make a charge for 'lending' a work where this is just to cover operating costs, even though 'lending' is defined as being where it does not involve direct or indirect economic or commercial advantage.

s 18A(5) says:

> Where lending by an establishment accessible to the public gives rise to a payment the amount of which does not go beyond what is necessary to cover the operating costs of the establishment, there is no direct or indirect economic or commercial advantage for the purposes of this section.
>
> Source: The National Archives, 2015

3.3.2.1   Public lending right

Section 40A of the CDPA 1988 provides the statutory authority required for public libraries to lend books, audiobooks or e-books. This applies where those items are covered by the public lending right scheme.

The Public Lending Right Scheme 1982 (Commencement of Variations) Order 2014: SI 2014/1457 brought into force on 1 July 2014 variations to the Scheme following the extension of the public lending right to narrators and producers and to audiobooks and e-books. A further Order was required – The Public Lending Right Scheme 1982 (Commencement of Variation and Amendment) Order 2014: SI 2014/1945 – to correct errors in SI 2014/1457. Remote downloading of e-books is not covered by the legislation at the moment.

Section 43 of the Digital Economy Act 2010 amends the Public Lending Right Act 1979 section 5(2). This uses the following definition of 'lent out':

(a)   means made available to a member of the public for use away from library premises for a limited time, but

(b)   does not include being communicated by means of electronic transmission to a place other than library premises,

and "loan" and "borrowed" are to be read accordingly;

"library premises" has the meaning given in section 8(7) of the Public Libraries and Museums Act 1964

"library premises" means —

(a)   any premises which are occupied by a library authority and are premises where library facilities are made available by the authority, in the course of their provision of a public library service, to members of the public;

(b)   any vehicle which is used by a library authority for the purpose of providing such a service and is a vehicle in which facilities are so made available.

Source: The National Archives, 2015

The Society of Authors has on numerous occasions raised concerns over whether the government are in breach of their obligations under the Rental and Lending Directive in light of the increasing reliance of local authorities on volunteers to run libraries because of the implications of these being exempt from remunerating authors for the lending of their works. In particular, the Society of Authors asks:

- how exempting volunteer libraries from PLR is in accord with the definition of 'public lending' in directive 2006/115/EC
- if it is intended that such exemption is a permitted derogation under Article 6 of the Directive, how that derogation could be considered proportionate or otherwise comply with Treaty obligations
- if volunteer libraries are exempted from being part of the statutory library service, how local authorities can comply with their legal obligation to provide a 'comprehensive and efficient' public library service as set out in section 7(1) of Public Libraries and Museums Act 1964.

There is no automatic right for public libraries to lend e-books remotely either in the legislation on copyright or that on public lending right. Many libraries do offer remote e-lending, but rely on this having been authorized by licence agreements. There is an international campaign entitled 'The Right to E-read' which is co-ordinated by the European Bureau of Library Information and Documentation Associations (EBLIDA) and supported by library organizations, including national library associations such as CILIP: the Chartered Institute for Library and Information Professionals. One of their aims is for the introduction of a mandatory exception granting libraries the right to lend – including remote e-lending – works in any format.

In addition to the s 40A exception on lending by publicly accessible libraries, there is also an exception covering lending of copies by educational establishments in s 36A of the CDPA 1988 (see Section 3.4.6 below).

What PLR does cover:

Printed books, audio books and e-books are eligible for PLR registration as long as:

- if the book is printed material that it is bound by a fixed cover
- it has been published
- copies of it have been offered for sale
- the authorship is personal
- it has an ISBN.

What PLR does not cover

- maps
- books which are wholly or mainly musical scores
- newspapers

- magazines
- journals
- Crown Copyright publications are not eligible for PLR in the UK or Ireland.

3.3.3   Making available content on dedicated terminals (s 40B)

The Copyright and Rights in Performances (Research, Education, Libraries and Archives) Regulations 2014: SI 2014/1372 inserted a provision into the Copyright, Designs and Patents Act 1988 which allows educational and cultural institutions (publicly accessible libraries, educational establishments, museums, galleries and archives) to make works available for research or private study via dedicated terminals on their premises. In educational establishments a university could, for example, install dedicated terminals within the university's library and language labs. The exception enables these institutions to provide enhanced access to cultural works that have been digitized. It can be used, for example, where the original works are too fragile to display.

The dedicated terminals exception relates to content which may be subject to purchase or licensing terms. So, what you will be able to do with the works you view on a dedicated terminal will be up to the licence terms of the work, and the facilities that are in place at the institution where you are viewing the work. The exception does not include a clause preventing contract override. The key points governing how this exception can be used are these:

- The work must have been lawfully acquired by the institution.
- It must be communicated or made available to individual members of the public for the purposes of research and private study.
- The work must be communicated or made available in compliance with any purchase or licensing terms to which it is subject.
- There is no clause preventing contract override.
- The access is limited to where it is on the premises of the institution at electronic terminals.

Technische Universität Darmstadt v Eugen Ulmer KG (CJEU Case C-117/13)

The European Court of Justice case Technische Universität Darmstadt v Eugen Ulmer clarifies how this exception works. What is clear from the case is that:

- Libraries can digitize books from their collections.
- Libraries cannot permit individuals to print out the works on paper or store them on a USB stick under the dedicated terminals exception.
- It would be possible for member states to use a different exception (using Article 5(2)(a) or (b)) to allow printing out of the work or storing it on a USB stick, but this would require fair compensation to be paid to the rights holders.

- The digitization of works by publicly accessible libraries in Germany cannot have the result that the number of copies of each work made available to users by dedicated terminals is greater than that which those libraries have acquired in analogue format, because that is what the German legislation says. Even if the UK's copyright legislation doesn't explicitly make the same stipulation, the UK's EU and international obligations require that the ancillary right of digitization does not conflict with the normal exploitation of the work and does not unreasonably prejudice the legitimate interests of the rights holder.

The acts of printing out a copy and of copying to a USB stick are both acts of reproduction. They are not an integral process which is required in order to be able to make the work available to the public.

The directive does not prevent member states from granting libraries the right to digitize the books from their collections, if their being made available to the public by dedicated terminals requires it. That may be the case where it is necessary to protect original works which, although still covered by copyright, are old, fragile or rare. That may also be the case where the work in question is consulted by a large number of students and its photocopying might result in disproportionate wear. The right of libraries to communicate, by dedicated terminals, the works they hold in their collections would risk being rendered largely meaningless, or indeed ineffective, if they did not have an ancillary right to digitize the works in question.

The directive does not permit the digitization of a collection in its entirety, but only the digitization of individual works. As a general rule and also in compliance with the three-step test in Article 5(5) of the same directive, the establishment in question may not digitize its entire collection.

It is particularly important not to opt to use dedicated terminals where the sole purpose of doing so is to avoid the purchase of a sufficient number of physical copies of the work.

In its final judgment in the Technische Universität Darmstadt v Eugen Ulmer KG case the CJEU held first of all, that, even if the rights holder offers to a library the possibility of concluding licensing agreements for the use of his works on appropriate terms, the library may avail itself of the exception provided for in favour of dedicated terminals; otherwise, the library could not realize its core mission or promote the public interest in promoting research and private study.

3.3.4   Supply of single copies to other libraries (s 41)

The regulations update section 41, which provides for an exception allowing libraries to make and supply copies of periodical articles and published literary, dramatic or musical works for the benefit of other libraries. They again extend the exception to apply to all types of published work. As with the previous law, this exception only applies when it is not possible to ascertain the name or address of a person entitled to authorize the making of the copy.

3.3.5   Copying for archiving and preservation (s 42)

The law has changed to make it easier for libraries, archives, museums and galleries to preserve their collections. These institutions are responsible for preserving our cultural heritage for the benefit of current and future generations. Preservation techniques often involve copying a cultural work or artefact – for example digitizing a book to transfer it to a more durable medium.

Libraries, archives, museums and galleries are now able to make copies of all types of creative works held in their permanent collections (but which are not available for loan to the public), in order to preserve them for future generations. This will ensure that our cultural heritage is not lost for future generations. The preservation exception is restricted to cases where it is not reasonably practicable to purchase a replacement copy.

The reason why the changes to the law were needed was because whilst the previous legislation allowed libraries and archives to make copies of books in order to preserve them, without infringing copyright, the previous law did not apply to standalone artistic works, sound recordings or films, nor did it previously apply to copying for preservation done by museums or galleries.

Under the revised wording of the preservation exception, libraries, museums and galleries are able to preserve films, broadcasts, sound recordings and artistic works (including photographs), as well as literary, dramatic and musical works. The work can be copied as many times as necessary for it to be preserved. It is necessary to allow multiple copies of works to be made for preservation/archiving because there is a risk that both the original and the copy of a work may degenerate over time. Making a single copy may be insufficient to safeguard a work in the long term. The legislative changes were needed because the previous wording wasn't suitable for preserving works in a digital age:

- It only allowed a single copy to be made, rather than permitting as many copies to be made as is necessary for the work to be preserved.
- It didn't cover all types of works, excluding categories such as standalone artistic works, sound recordings, films and broadcasts.
- It didn't allow format shifting.

All of these issues have been addressed and resolved by the new wording of the section 42 exception.

3.3.6   Copying by librarians: single copies of published works (s 42A)

Librarians are permitted to assist researchers and students by providing limited copies of works for non-commercial research and private study. The amount that can be copied is restricted to a reasonable proportion. It is worthy of note that these exceptions now cover all types of copyright works. Library staff can copy for a user:

- one article in any one issue of a periodical; or
- a reasonable proportion of any other published work (see s 42A).

Libraries and archives are also now able to make copies of artistic works for researchers and students. Previously there was an anomaly whereby researchers and students could copy artistic works under fair dealing, but where librarians could not do the same copying on their behalf. That anomaly has now been removed.

This provision is subject to a number of conditions:

- The copy has to be supplied in response to a request from a person who has provided the librarian with a written declaration (see Section 3.3.8 and Figures 3.2 and 3.3 below).
- The librarian is not aware that the declaration is false in a material particular.
- No charge is required, but where a charge is made this should be calculated based on the costs attributable to the production of the copy.
- No contract can prevent or restrict this from being so.

3.3.7   Copying by librarians or archivists: single copies of unpublished works (s 43)

Librarians or archivists can make and supply single copies of either the whole or a part of a work provided that:

- the copy is in response to a user request
- the user has completed a declaration in writing (and this must contain certain information specified in section 43(2))
- the work has not been published or communicated to the public before the date it was deposited in the library or archive
- the copyright owner has not prohibited the copying of the work.

The section 43 exception can only be used if the work has not been published or communicated to the public before the date it was deposited in the library or archive and the copyright owner has not prohibited the copying of the work in circumstances where the librarian or archivist is, or ought to be, aware of that fact at the time of making the copy.

There is no requirement for the library or archive to impose a charge for the making of the copy. But in circumstances where a charge is made, the sum charged must be calculated by reference to the costs attributable to the production of the copy.

3.3.8   Copyright declarations

Librarians[4] working in not-for-profit publicly accessible libraries can copy on behalf of their users a single copy of:

- one article in any one issue of a periodical; or
- a reasonable proportion of any other published work (which generally means that only a limited part that is necessary for the research or study purpose may be copied) or
- the whole or part of an unpublished work (provided the owner of that work has not prohibited the copying of that work).

The conditions under which this is possible are that

- the copy is supplied in response to a request from a person who has provided the librarian with a declaration in writing
- the librarian is not aware that the declaration is false in any material form.

The provisions are set out in the following sections of the CDPA 1988:

- Section 42A, Copying by librarians: single copies of published works
- Section 43, Copying by librarians or archivists: single copies of unpublished works.

The written confirmation can be submitted electronically, which is in line with the government's Digital by Default strategy. If the requestor makes a false declaration, it is the requestor rather than the librarian who infringes copyright.

The copyright declaration forms provide librarians with an indemnity. It is important to retain the completed forms for six years plus the current year in view of the Limitation Act 1980.

The revised legislation regarding declaration forms means that a signature is no longer required on the forms. Where library users make requests remotely – such as by telephone or by e-mail – it is not necessary to get them to put a signed declaration form in the post before a copy is supplied. Instead the declaration form can be sent to the user by e-mail requesting that they fill in their name details on the form (and this can be typed, it doesn't require a digital signature) and the user can send the completed declaration form back to the library by e-mail.

The forms do not have to conform to the standard declaration form. However, the legislation does stipulate what information they must contain (see section 42A(3) for the making of single copies of published works and section 43(2) for the making of copies of unpublished works).

The information which must be included in the declaration is:

1 the name of the person who requires the copy and the material which that person requires

2 a statement that the person has not previously been supplied with a copy of that material by any library (or, in the case of unpublished works, by any library or archive)

3 a statement that the person requires the copy for the purposes of research for a non-commercial purpose or private study, will use it only for those purposes and will not supply the copy to any other person, and

4 (only in the case of single copies of published works, a further stipulation that the declaration contains) a statement that to the best of the person's knowledge, no other person with whom the person works or studies has made, or intends to make, at or about the same time as the person's request, a request for substantially the same material for substantially the same purpose. (Source: IPO, 2015)

Declaration forms are also required where librarians supply users on request with single copies of published recordings (Schedule 2 (6F)), and unpublished recordings (Schedule 2 (6G)); single copies of sound recordings of folk songs (s61), and recordings of folk songs (Schedule 2 (14)).

Figures 3.2 and 3.3 are examples of declaration forms for copying published and unpublished works.

DECLARATION: COPY OF ARTICLE OR PART OF PUBLISHED WORK
To: The Librarian of [..] Library [Address of Library]

1. Please supply me with a copy of*
The article in the periodical, the particulars of which are ....
....
The reasonable portion of the published work, the particulars of which are ....
....
required by me for the purposes of non-commercial research or private study.

2. I declare that:
   a) I have not previously been supplied with a copy of the same material by you or any other librarian;
   b) I will not use the copy except for research for a non-commercial purpose or private study and will not supply the copy to any other person; and
   c) to the best of my knowledge, no other person with whom I work or study has made or intends to make, at or about the same time as this request, a request for substantially the same material for substantially the same purpose.

3. I understand that if the declaration is false in a material particular, the copy supplied to me by you will be an infringing copy, and that I shall be liable for infringement of copyright as if I had made the copy myself.

Date...
NAME...
ADDRESS...
....
....
* Delete whichever is inappropriate

Figure 3.2 *Model declaration form: copy of article or part of published work*

DECLARATION: COPY OF WHOLE OR PART OF UNPUBLISHED WORK
To: The Librarian/Archivist* of [...] Library/Archive*
[Address of Library/Archive]

1. Please supply me with a copy of
The whole/following part* [particulars of part] of the [particulars of the unpublished
work] required by me for the purposes of non-commercial research or private study.

2. I declare that:
   a) I have not previously been supplied with a copy of the same material by you or any
   other librarian or archivist;
   b) I will not use the copy except for research for a non-commercial purpose or
   private study and will not supply the copy to any other person; and
   c) to the best of my knowledge the work had not been published before the
   document was deposited in your library/archive* and the copyright owner has not
   prohibited copying of the work.

3. I understand that if the declaration is false in a material particular, the copy supplied to
me by you will be an infringing copy, and that I shall be liable for infringement of
copyright as if I had made the copy myself.

Date...
NAME..
ADDRESS...
....
....
*Delete whichever is inappropriate

Figure 3.3 *Model declaration form: copy of whole or part of unpublished work*

3.3.9   Charging library users

Libraries now have the flexibility to determine whether or not they charge students and researchers for making and supplying copies, but any charge must be in line with the cost of making and supplying that copy. I don't think that differential charging (whereby you charge one group of users a different amount from another group of users) could be justified, because the charge needs to be tied in with the cost of producing the copy. Charging for a copy is not obligatory but if a charge is made it needs to be based on a cost recovery calculation.

3.4   Educational exceptions

The changes to copyright law introduced by The Copyright and Rights in Performances (Research, Education, Libraries and Archives) Regulations 2014: SI 2014/1372 bring the education exceptions up to date, and they reflect advances in digital technology. They allow teachers and lecturers to use copyright works with modern teaching equipment without risk of copyright infringement, and they also remove administrative burdens from schools and universities. Table 3.3 on the next page summarizes the educational exceptions.

Table 3.3 *Summary of the educational exceptions*

Section number in the CDPA 1988	Name of the exception	Is it only available for the benefit of educational establishments?	Is it only available to the extent that there aren't educational licensing schemes available to authorize the acts of copying?	What are the amount limits?
Section 32	Illustration for instruction	NO	NO	Fair dealing
Section 33	Anthologies for educational use	YES	NO	No more than two excerpts from copyright works by the same author in collections published by the same publisher over any period of five years
Section 34	Performing, playing or showing work in the course of activities of educational establishment	YES	NO	No amount limit specified
Section 35	Recording by educational establishments of broadcasts	YES	YES	No amount limit specified
Section 36	Copying and use of extracts of works by educational establishments	YES	YES	No more than 5% per year
Section 36A	Lending of copies by educational establishments	YES	NO	No amount limit specified

British copyright law has long included exceptions for education. In the Copyright Act 1956, for example, section 41 covered use of copyright material for education. The fact that the UK's copyright legislation has had educational exceptions for many years is a recognition of the fact that copying is often a necessary part of teaching and that people learn through analysing, imitating and reproducing the works of others.

There isn't a general educational exception which acts as a 'catch-all' exception to authorize all educational uses of materials. Instead, there are half a dozen exceptions each of which is narrowly defined and each of which sets out the conditions or restrictions applicable to that specific exception. The six exceptions which can be grouped together as 'educational exceptions' are:

- s 32, Illustration for instruction (see Section 3.4.1 below)
- s 33, Anthologies for educational use (see Section 3.4.2)
- s 34, Performing, playing or showing work in course of activities of educational establishment (see Section 3.4.3)
- s 35, Recording by educational establishments of broadcasts (see Section 3.4.4)
- s 36, Copying and use of extracts of works by educational establishments (see Section 3.4.5)
- s 36A, Lending of copies by educational establishments (see Section 3.4.6)

In June 2014 copyright law was modernized by The Copyright and Rights in Performances (Research, Education, Libraries and Archives) Regulations (SI 2014/1372) to make it easier for schools, colleges and universities to use copyright materials. It amended the wording of the CDPA 1988 to remove restrictions on the use of copyright materials with modern teaching practices such as distance learning or the use of interactive whiteboards.

The section 32 fair dealing exception which permits copying for the purpose of illustration for instruction applies to acts of teaching in general, and it is not restricted to teaching undertaken solely by educational establishments (for further details of the section 32 exception, see Section 3.2.3 above). All of the other five educational exceptions are only intended for the benefit of educational establishments, and the types of educational providers which can be considered to be 'educational establishments' for the purposes of the CDPA 1988 are specified in The Copyright (Educational Establishments) Order 2005 SI 2005/223. The definition of educational establishments covers higher education, further education and theological colleges. For the full definition it is best to consult the statutory instrument at www.legislation.gov.uk/uksi/2005/223/contents/made.

Two of the education exceptions (section 35, on the recording of broadcasts and section 36, on copying from published works) are only available in the absence of an educational licensing scheme. Both sections use the following form of words to express this limitation on the scope or extent to which the exceptions can be relied upon:

Acts which would otherwise be permitted by this section are not permitted if, or to the extent that, licences are available authorizing the acts in question and the educational establishment responsible for those acts knew or ought to have been aware of that fact.

Source: The National Archives, 2015

In the case of section 35, on the recording of broadcasts, if for example a college wanted to record television broadcasts for classroom use, they would need to get a licence from the Educational Recording Agency.

The aim of the changes introduced in June 2014 (by SI 2014/1372) is to simplify the law. In its guidance on the education exceptions (IPO, 2014), the IPO states that:

> These licensing schemes are underpinned by copyright exceptions which mean that, where a particular work is not covered by a licence, an educational establishment is still able to copy it. This means that teachers do not have to check the terms of each item they want to copy before they copy it.
>
> *Exceptions to Copyright: education and teaching,* IPO, March 2014

The IPO statement makes it sound so easy, because if it is not covered by a licence, you can copy it under the exception.

The section 36 exception covers copying and use of extracts from published works by educational establishments. But:

- it does not cover broadcasts (as they are covered by section 35), nor does it cover standalone artistic works
- it only permits a maximum of 5% of the work being copied within any 12-month period
- all of this is only permitted to the extent that there aren't any licences available to authorize the copying in question.

The most fundamental problem with being able to use the section 36 exception is that you would need to be confident that no more than 5% of the work had been copied by the educational establishment as a whole during the course of a 12-month period, and one has to ask whether that is feasible without creating a Big Brother surveillance and monitoring operation to ensure that all instances of copying are recorded.

3.4.1   Illustration for instruction (s 32)

Section 32 of the CDPA 1988 permits fair dealing for the purpose of illustration for instruction. It is distinct from the other educational copying exceptions because while the exceptions in sections 33–36A are only intended for use by educational establishments, the section 32 fair dealing exception applies to acts of teaching in general, and it is not restricted to teaching undertaken by educational establishments. It would, for example, cover other providers of instruction such as museums and youth organizations.

Under the section 32 exception teachers are able to copy a small amount of material where it is necessary to illustrate a point, without first having to seek permission from the copyright owner. For example, a teacher would be able to reproduce a few lines of poetry or a few bars of musical notation on an interactive whiteboard and students would be able to copy down the example using a laptop. However, uses which would undermine sales of teaching materials would require a licence.

The section 32 fair dealing exception allows copying of works in any medium as long as all the following conditions apply:

1 The work must be used solely to illustrate a point.
2 The use of the work must not be for commercial purposes.
3 The use must be fair dealing.
4 It must be accompanied by a sufficient acknowledgement.

It applies to dealing with a work:

* by a person giving or receiving instruction, or
* by a person preparing for giving or receiving instruction, or
* in order to set examination questions (see Section 3.4.1.3 below).

3.4.1.1   What does the exception cover?

Provided the various conditions are met (that the use is necessary in order to illustrate or reinforce a teaching point, that the use is fair dealing with the work, and that it is accompanied by a sufficient acknowledgement), the section 32 exception would cover:

* placing a work onto a virtual learning environment where this was used as illustration for instruction
* use of images in a PowerPoint presentation published to the VLE
* inclusion of third-party material which is captured in the recording of a lecture.

3.4.1.2   Fair dealing

The section 32 exception is limited to fair dealing in the work. There are a number of measures which can be taken so that the use is fair.

* Use low-resolution images rather than high-resolution images.
* Limit the amount of time that the material is available. It would be possible, for example, to ensure that the copy of the work is only available for the duration of the course.
* Consider who has access to the VLE when assessing whether or not the use is

fair. Restrict access to the students who are enrolled on the specific course in question.
- The use of the work must not negatively impact the market for the original materials.
- The amount used must be limited to that which is strictly necessary to illustrate a point.

Bear in mind that every case is different, and each instance of copying would need to be considered based on the specific factors involved in that particular act of copying.

Permitting students to download materials increases the risk of a subsequent use being made of the work which adversely affects the rights holder. This risk can be addressed by giving clear guidance as to the purpose for which students are permitted to download and use the materials.

Use of this exception to justify copying from a work for an open course available as a MOOC could be problematic if the content is provided openly online to anyone who registers for the MOOC (see Figure 3.4).

The whole point of MOOCs is that they are 'massively open' and the students who register for them come from a wide range of countries.

There are copyright risks associated with MOOCs because they will often consist of a compilation of materials from multiple contributors.

Institutions should check the terms and conditions of the MOOC provider to see whether they seek rights from them such as the right of redistribution, and even the right of resale.

Students usually enrol or register with the MOOC platform provider, rather than having a direct relationship with the educational establishment providing the course materials for the MOOC, and so it would not be possible to rely on the educational institution's CLA licence.

To avoid copyright problems with material you wish to use in a MOOC:

- create your own original materials
- use open access materials
- seek permission to use third-party content.

Copyright is a territorial right, and different acts are permitted in different countries. The wording of the new education exceptions do not authorize the provision of online courses to people in other countries. Rather, you would need to ensure that you comply with the laws of the countries in which you provide the online resources (see also the end of Section 1.3 on pp. 3–5, which deals with the recognition of foreign copyright works and performances) and where necessary to get the copying authorized or licensed.

Figure 3.4 *Copyright and MOOCs*

Where a purely commercial course is being provided, those giving or receiving instruction on the course cannot benefit from the exception because it only covers non-commercial research or private study.

Some people requested clarification that the section 32 exception on illustration for instruction would cover post-examination uses such as reproducing exam questions in preparatory material. The government's view is that such use is likely to be considered fair dealing and so would be permitted by this exception where the use made is minimal, non-commercial and fair.

As was the case before the section 32 exception was amended in 2014, schools will still need photocopying licences in order to reproduce sheet music, for use by orchestras, for example (these are available from Printed Music Licensing Limited which is owned by the Music Publishers Association). The fair dealing exception will only allow small, illustrative uses, such as copying and displaying a few bars of musical notation to a class studying musical composition.

3.4.1.3   Copying for exams

The illustration for instruction exception can be used where copying is done for examination purposes. Section 32(2) makes clear that 'giving or receiving instruction' includes the setting of examination questions, communicating the questions to pupils and answering the questions.

Teachers can rely on the exception if they want to reproduce a piece of text for analysis in an English exam, for example. However, the amount that can be copied is subject to fair dealing. Potentially they could also rely on the quotation exception (CDPA s 30 – see Section 3.2.5) to copy material for use in exams – such as where they reproduce a piece of text or analysis in an English exam, although the quotation exception is also subject to fair dealing.

The wording of section 32 used to say that:

> Copyright is not infringed by *anything done for the purposes of an examination* by way of setting the questions, communicating the questions to the candidates or answering the questions, provided that the questions are accompanied by a sufficient acknowledgement. [My italics]

However, the current wording of the section 32 exception on illustration for instruction is undoubtedly more restrictive because it is subject to the fair dealing test:

(1)   Fair dealing with a work for the sole purpose of illustration for instruction does not infringe copyright in the work provided that the dealing is—

    (a)   for a non-commercial purpose,

    (b)   by a person giving or receiving instruction (or preparing for giving or receiving instruction), and

    (c)   accompanied by a sufficient acknowledgement (unless this would be impossible for reasons of practicality or otherwise).

(2) For the purposes of subsection (1), "giving or receiving instruction" includes setting examination questions, communicating the questions to pupils and answering the questions . . .

Source: IPO, 2014

As a result, where material is copied for educational purposes (including examination purposes), people giving or receiving instruction (which includes those setting examination questions) now have to weigh up whether or not the copying that they are planning to undertake can be said to be fair and reasonable, asking themselves the following questions:

- Is it for an educational purpose (in the case of examinations, for the setting of the questions, communicating the questions to the students, or answering the questions)?
- Is it accompanied by a proper acknowledgement?
- Is the amount being used strictly necessary for the educational/examination purpose?
- Is the dissemination of the content limited or restricted (for example by being on a secure network)?
- Are you confident that it will not prejudice the legitimate interests of the rights holder, and that it will not damage their ability to exploit their content?

3.4.1.4 Theses

Theses may include material for which the copyright is held by a third party. The section 32 copyright exception has been used to justify copying of such material within theses. However, the revised wording means that this type of copying is now subject to the fair dealing test. The sorts of things that could be problematic include:

- maps such as those from Google Maps or the Ordnance Survey
- photographs that weren't taken by the student who wrote the thesis
- third-party tables or charts
- material which the student has previously had published in which he or she has signed the rights over to a journal publisher.

E-theses are accessed many more times by people around the world than printed theses and so the copyright risks are higher. They are much more highly visible than their print counterparts. Indeed, a number of publishers regularly monitor sites for new theses with a view to finding ones which they would like to publish commercially. Some elements of a thesis may need to be removed for copyright reasons before they are made available electronically.

Universities have thesis deposit forms or deposit agreements which often require students to complete a declaration which includes a statement regarding copyright. For example:

> I have read the library's guidelines on third-party copyright and understand the importance of obtaining rights holders' permissions before agreeing that my thesis can be made publicly available online through xyz institution's repository.

Students can include third-party copyright material in their thesis or dissertation under the illustration for instruction exception (s 32) provided that it is for the purposes of assessment. However, this exception is subject to the fairness test, and it doesn't mean that the thesis can automatically be made freely available online.

Theses often comprise an important part of an institutional repository and there are electronic collections of theses such as the British Library's national online theses portal EthOS (http://ethos.bl.uk).

A useful resource is *Keeping Your Thesis Legal*, University of Leicester, 2014, v2.4. ★ Original text by Gareth Johnson, Tania Rowlett and Rob Melocha. Amended and updated by Tania Rowlett and Brett Dodgson.

3.4.2   Anthologies for educational use (s 33)

It is possible to include a short passage from a published literary or dramatic work in a collection as long as this is intended for use by educational establishments and is described as such in its title and in any advertisements issued by or on behalf of the publisher.

There are a number of qualifiers which clarify or limit the extent to which the exception can be relied upon:

- The inclusion of the short passage should be accompanied by a sufficient acknowledgement.
- The use of the work should be for the educational purposes of the educational establishment.
- No more than two pieces of a copyright work by the same author can be included in an anthology within a five-year period, and then only provided sufficient acknowledgement is given.
- The material in the anthology consists mainly of material in which no copyright subsists.

3.4.3   Performing, playing or showing a work in the course of activities of educational establishments (s 34)

The section 34 exception covers:

- the performance of a literary, dramatic or musical work
- the playing or showing of a sound recording, film or broadcast.

The exception only permits the use of the work to the extent that:

- the audience consists of teachers and pupils at the educational establishment and others who are directly connected with the activities of the establishment
- the performance or the playing/showing of the work is undertaken by either a teacher or a pupil in the course of the activities of the establishment or by anyone at the establishment for the purposes of instruction.

Section 34 subsection 3 does make clear that a person is not considered to be directly connected with the educational establishment merely by being a parent of a pupil at the establishment.

Educational establishments such as schools and universities still need licences for activities such as photocopying books and articles and recording broadcasts. The new laws do not change the need for schools, universities and colleges to have those licences in place. Many schools, colleges and universities copy media which is protected by copyright – for instance, photocopying extracts from books for class handouts or recording television programmes to show to a class. In order to do this, educational establishments must hold educational copying licences. So if a school wants to record television broadcasts, it needs a licence from the Educational Recording Agency. If it wants to photocopy extracts from books, it needs a licence from the Copyright Licensing Agency. Most educational establishments already hold these licences.

If a licence was granted before the new laws came into force, and permits a wider range of activities than the new laws, then it will be unaffected. Conversely, if the new laws let you do more than your licence, then you can rely on the new laws. Your licence will still be valid, but if it says you cannot use a copyright work in a way permitted by the new laws, you can use the work under the exception without infringing copyright.

These licensing schemes are underpinned by copyright exceptions which mean that, where a particular work is not covered by a licence, an educational establishment is still able to copy it. This means that teachers do not have to check the terms of each item they want to copy before they copy it.

3.4.4   Recording of broadcasts (s 35)

The previous wording of section 35 permitted educational establishments to record broadcasts for educational purposes, and to play those recordings before an audience within the school premises. If a licence scheme certified by the Secretary of State was available for this activity, an establishment was required to hold that licence and could not rely on the exception. The amendments made by the 2014 regulations (SI 2014/1372) no longer require that the licensing scheme must be certified by the Secretary of State. Another key point about the 2014 regulations is that they revise the wording of the section 35 exception to reflect the fact that education increasingly takes place outside the classroom or lecture theatre, using virtual learning environments. Sections 35 and 36 both use the phrase 'secure electronic network'. So access to recordings can be made by students on secure networks such as Moodle or Blackboard. The exception now covers the communication of the recordings of broadcasts by educational establishments outside the premises of the establishment, but only where this is done through the use of a *secure electronic network* which is only accessible by the establishment's pupils and staff. So the exception applies to virtual classrooms to the same extent as it applies to real ones, thereby making it easier for teachers to use distance learning technology.

Section 27 of the CDPA 1988 says that an article is an infringing copy if 'its making in the United Kingdom would have constituted an infringement of the copyright in the work in question, or a breach of an exclusive licence agreement relating to that work'. And it spells out that an 'infringing copy' would include a copy failing to be treated as an infringing copy by virtue of section 35(5) (recording by educational establishments of broadcasts). Section 35(5) says:

> If a copy made under this section is subsequently dealt with—
> (a) it is to be treated as an infringing copy for the purposes of that dealing, and
> (b) if that dealing infringes copyright, it is to be treated as an infringing copy for all subsequent purposes
>
> Source: IPO, 2014

Section 35(4) says that:

> Acts which would otherwise be permitted by this section are not permitted if, or to the extent that, licences are available authorizing the acts in question and the educational establishment responsible for those acts knew or ought to have been aware of that fact
>
> Source: IPO, 2014

The Educational Recording Agency operates a licensing scheme on behalf of its 20 members for educational use of broadcast material both in the classroom and by students at home. For more details about the ERA licence see Section 4.6.4 below.

3.4.5   Copying and use of extracts of works (s 36)

A teacher is able to make copies of extracts from works without worrying about copyright infringement, as long as they (and their establishment) copy no more than 5% of the work per annum; but this only relates to instances where the material is not covered by a licence, because if that is the case, the educational establishment would need to take out the relevant licence.

The old section 36 exception permitted educational establishments to make reprographic copies of passages from works. For example, it permitted a teacher to make photocopies of pages of course books for inclusion in handouts to their class. As with the exception for recording broadcasts, where a relevant licence is available (such as the CLA photocopying licence) an educational establishment was required to hold it to carry out this activity.

The 2014 regulations amend section 36 so that it is no longer confined to certain types of copyright work, but applies to all types of work (apart, that is, from broadcasts, and artistic works that are not incorporated into other works).

Educational licences are available for categories of works such as:

- books, journals and magazines: Copyright Licensing Agency
- newspapers and magazines: NLA Media Access
- printed music: Printed Music Licensing Ltd (which offers, for example, a schools printed music licence).

The copying limit contained in section 36 was raised from 1% of a work per quarter to 5% of a work per annum. Another change is that teachers are allowed to distribute copies via secure electronic networks.

Section 36 is quite difficult to apply in practice because the 5% limit per year means that the total copying undertaken by the entire educational establishment must not go beyond that amount. Therefore the establishment would need to have measures in place to record *all* of the copying undertaken in order to ensure that it had stayed within the 5% limit per year.

3.4.6   Lending of copies by educational establishments (s 36A)

Rental and lending of works is a restricted act under section 16(1)(BA) of CDPA 1988. The wording of this section 36A is quite short. It simply states that:

> Copyright in a work is not infringed by the lending of copies of the work by an educational establishment

> Source: The National Archives, 2015

The sheer simplicity of the wording does mean that there are no limits to the type of work covered by the exception; and this is in contrast with the section 40A exception on the lending of copies by libraries or archives, which is linked to the Public Lending Right Act 1979, and as such covers only the types of works which are covered by public lending right.

3.5   Public administration

3.5.1   Parliamentary and judicial proceedings (s 45)

The wording of the exception is:

> Parliamentary and judicial proceedings
>
> (1)   Copyright is not infringed by anything done for the purposes of parliamentary or judicial proceedings.
>
> (2)   Copyright is not infringed by anything done for the purposes of reporting such proceedings; but this shall not be construed as authorising the copying of a work which is itself a published report of the proceedings.
>
> Source: The National Archives, 2015

Definitions of the terms judicial proceedings and parliamentary proceedings are given in section 178 of the CDPA:

> 'judicial proceedings' includes proceedings before any court, tribunal or person having authority to decide any matter affecting a person's legal rights or liabilities;
>
> 'parliamentary proceedings' includes proceedings of the Northern Ireland Assembly of the Scottish Parliament or of the European Parliament and Assembly proceedings within the meaning of section 1(5) of the Government of Wales Act 2006
>
> Source: The National Archives, 2015

3.5.2   Royal Commissions and statutory inquiries (s 46)

Copyright is not infringed by anything done for the purposes of the proceedings of a Royal Commission or statutory inquiry; the reporting of any such proceedings held in public; and the issue to the public of copies of the report of a Royal Commission or statutory inquiry containing the work or material from it. The phrases 'Royal Commission' and 'statutory inquiry' are defined as:

> "Royal Commission" includes a Commission appointed for Northern Ireland by the Secretary of State in pursuance of the prerogative powers of Her Majesty delegated to him[/her] under section 7(2) of the Northern Ireland Constitution Act 1973; and
>
> "Statutory inquiry" means an inquiry held or investigation conducted in pursuance of a duty imposed or power conferred by or under an enactment
>
> Source: The National Archives, 2015

3.5.3   Material open to public inspection or on an official register (s 47)

Section 47(1) says

> Where material is open to public inspection pursuant to a statutory requirement, or is on a statutory register, any copyright in the material as a literary work is not infringed by the copying of so much of the material as contains factual information of any description, by or with the authority of the appropriate person, for a purpose which does not involve the issuing of copies to the public.
>
> Source: IPO, 2014

There were a number of changes made by The Copyright (Public Administration) Regulations 2014: SI 2014/1385. Sections 47 (Material open to public inspection or on official register) and 48 (Material communicated to the Crown in the course of public business) contain exceptions to copyright in respect of the copying and issue to members of the public of documents which are open to public inspection or on an official register and of material which is communicated to the Crown in the course of public business. The amendments made by SI 2014/1385 extend the exceptions so as to permit the relevant public bodies to publish the material on the internet so that members of the public may access it online.

Some material held by public bodies will have been submitted, for example, by businesses or members of the public. This could be material submitted to a public body, such as a local authority, as part of a duty to capture information required for a public register. Public bodies were previously only able to provide that material by issuing paper copies or making the material available for inspection at their premises. Making this material available for wider viewing on the internet now enables the public to access information easily and conveniently.

At a time when the government's Digital by Default strategy encourages public bodies to provide information via the internet, the old system was outmoded and had the potential to generate repeated written requests for the same material. Making such third-party material available online therefore has the potential to reduce administrative costs for public bodies, thereby saving public money and time. The change also improves transparency and public confidence in government and other public bodies.

The change only applies to material that is already available for public inspection through some statutory mechanism or material that is unpublished. However, it does not apply to material which the copyright owner has made available on a commercial basis (for example publications which carry a cover charge), as this would not meet the 'three-step test' which appears in both the Berne Convention of 1886 and the Copyright Directive 2001/29/EC, because it might conflict with the copyright owner's right to exploit the material if it were to be placed on the internet.

If a public body wanted to publish material that is commercially available to buy or license (such as academic articles), it would still need to seek the permission of the rights holder.

The changes only give the new powers to the public body or registrar, not to members of the public. Anyone accessing information shared by the public body remains bound by the usual copyright rules, ensuring material is properly protected. The exception does not, therefore, substantively affect the ability of rights holders to control copies of their work, nor does it pose any risk to their revenue.

Public bodies can include on their websites certain third-party copyright material in which someone other than the public body owns the copyright, e.g. businesses and members of the public. They are also permitted to share that material through e-mail, as well as the existing mechanism of issuing paper copies.

The change to the law grants permission to public bodies to publish material online, but only:

- where that material is on a statutory register; or
- where it is already open to public inspection; or
- where it has been communicated to the Crown for a purpose which reasonably justifies further dissemination.

It does not create a requirement for any particular material to be published online. It is a mechanism to help avoid having to respond to repeat requests for similar material. Public bodies are already encouraged to publish material on their websites, so are likely to have the infrastructure for doing this.

It is important to note that any material that is published online by a public body continues to be protected by copyright and as a result the law prevents the public from making further copies of the material.

3.5.4   Material communicated to the Crown in the course of public business (s 48)

The wording of this exception has been changed to enable the making available of a work by electronic transmission. The exception now reads as follows:

(1)   This section applies where a literary, dramatic, musical or artistic work has in the course of public business been communicated to the Crown for any purpose, by or with the licence of the copyright owner and a document or other material thing recording or embodying the work is owned by or in the custody or control of the Crown.

(2)   The Crown may, without infringing copyright in the work, do an act specified in subsection (3) provided that —

     (a)   the act is done for the purpose for which the work was communicated to the Crown, or any related purpose which could reasonably have been anticipated by the copyright owner, and

     (b)   the work has not been previously published otherwise than by virtue of this section.

  (3)   The acts referred to in subsection (2) are—

     (a)   copying the work,

     (b)   issuing copies of the work to the public, and

     (c)   making the work (or a copy of it) available to the public by electronic transmission in such a way that members of the public may access it from a place and at a time individually chosen by them.

Source: IPO, 2014

3.5.5   Public records (s 49)

Material which is contained in public records within the meaning of the Public Records Act 1958, the Public Records (Scotland) Act 1937 or the Public Records Act (Northern Ireland) 1923, or in Welsh public records (as defined in the Government of Wales Act 2006), which are open to public inspection in pursuance of that Act, may be copied, and a copy may be supplied to any person, by or with the authority of any officer appointed under that Act, without infringement of copyright.

Where copying is permitted this should be interpreted as meaning it can be copied in any material form, which would include making electronic copies. Unless the Act contains limiting language, the terminology should be interpreted broadly to include any relevant form, so that copying, without anything to qualify or narrow the term, means any form of copying. An electronic copy made under s 49 may be supplied to the reader. Public records that are open to public inspection are covered by the revised wording of section 47(2).

3.5.6   Acts done under statutory authority (s 50)

There is an exception in section 50 for acts which are done under statutory authority. This states:

50 Acts done under statutory authority

(1)   Where the doing of a particular act is specifically authorised by an Act of Parliament, whenever passed, then, unless the Act provides otherwise, the doing of that act does not infringe copyright.

(2)   Subsection (1) applies in relation to an enactment contained in Northern Ireland legislation as it applies in relation to an Act of Parliament.

(3) Nothing in this section shall be construed as excluding any defence of statutory authority otherwise available under or by virtue of any enactment.

Source: The National Archives, 2015

My understanding of the section is that where another Act of Parliament authorizes copying to be undertaken, the CDPA 1988 would not try to override such an authorization.

The exceptions are intended to be narrowly drawn, and so as with any exception it should not be used as a general heading within which to justify a wide range of copying activity. In other words, the copying must be necessary for the performance of the function specified (by any such Act of Parliament) and must not be used to justify the copying of material merely because it would be nice to have.

The Freedom of Information Act 2000 (FOIA) doesn't explicitly authorize the copying of a piece of information in order to fulfil a request made under the Act (FOI request). What it specifies is the right of public access to information held by public authorities, and there are various ways in which the right could be fulfilled – by providing a summary of the information, by letting a member of the public inspect the item at the public authority's offices, etc. However:

- Both the CDPA 1988 and the Copyright and Rights in Database Regulations 1997 provide that IP rights will not be infringed where an act is authorized by an Act of Parliament.
- Responding to an FOI request is an act authorized by parliament.
- This has been interpreted to mean that disclosures under FOIA will not infringe IP rights.

However, in this particular example, even where the information is copied and supplied to the person making the FOI request that information is still protected by copyright. Public authorities are required to provide FOI responses based upon the information that they hold, and it may well mean that the intellectual property rights in some of the information held by them belongs to a third party. Where that is so, the public authority doesn't own the copyrights and it makes sense for the authority to draw the attention of members of the public to the existence of those rights.

Guidance from the Information Commissioner's Office (*Intellectual Property Rights and Disclosures Under The Freedom Of Information Act*, ICO, 2012) says that 'the existence of IP rights is not a valid reason for refusing to communicate information via an e-mail address which would result in the automatic publication of the material on a website'.

3.6   Other exceptions

This section covers exceptions for:

- computer programs (Section 3.6.1 below)
- databases (3.6.2)
- data mining (3.6.3)
- the making of temporary copies (3.6.4)
- the making of accessible copies for disabled persons (3.6.5)
- personal copies for private use (3.6.6).

3.6.1   Computer programs (ss 50A–50C)

Section 3 of the CDPA 1988 includes computer programs and preparatory design material for a computer program within the definition of a 'literary work'. Sections 50A–50C of the CDPA set out a number of exceptions relating to computer programs:

- Section 50A enables a lawful user of a computer program to make a back-up copy where it is necessary for him/her to have a back-up for the purposes of his lawful use.
- Section 50B enables a lawful user of a computer program to decompile it, subject to conditions.
- Section 50BA enables a lawful user of a computer program to observe, study or test the functionality of the program in order to determine the ideas and principles underlying any element of the program.
- Section 50C enables a lawful user of a computer program to copy or adapt it, subject to conditions (and these are that 'it is necessary to decompile the program to obtain the information necessary to create an independent program which can be operated with the program decompiled or with another program and the information is not used for any other purpose').

Sections 50A, 50B and 50BA covering activities relating to computer programs specify that they cannot be overridden by the terms of a contract.

The section 28B exception on the making of personal copies for private use specifically excludes computer programs from being within its scope. This is because at the time of the passing of the personal copies for private use exception (by SI 2014/2361), the computer programs exceptions already enabled copies to be made for back-up and lawful use.

Computer programs are excluded from the moral right to be identified as the author (section 77) or the moral right to object to a derogatory treatment of a work (section 80).

3.6.2   Databases (s 50D)

A person who has a right to use a database – whether under a licence or otherwise – is entitled to do anything in the exercise of that right which is necessary to access and use the contents of the database. This exception cannot be overridden by a contract. So, a lawful user of a database cannot be prevented by contract from being able to copy insubstantial portions of the database. There is a definition of database in section 3A of the CDPA 1988:

> "database" means a collection of independent works, data or other materials which –
> (a)   are arranged in a systematic or methodical way, and
> (b)   are individually accessible by electronic or other means.

Source: The National Archives, 2015

In other words, a database need not necessarily be in electronic form. The definition could, for example, include printed reference books. Section 3A also says that a literary work consisting of a database is original if, and only if, by reason of the selection or arrangement of the contents of the database the database constitutes the author's own intellectual creation.

3.6.3   Data mining (s 29A)

Data mining techniques can help researchers to analyse the huge amounts of data and information that are now being produced, and to do so more effectively than would otherwise be the case.

The copying exception for the purposes of data and text analysis which is contained in section 29A of the CDPA 1988 only applies when the research is being undertaken for non-commercial purposes. Indeed, there are a number of conditions which apply to the data mining exception. They include the following requirements:

- It applies where the research is for a non-commercial purpose.
- The person must have lawful access to the work (whether under licence or otherwise).
- The exception cannot be overridden by contract.
- It is subject to proper attribution, unless this would be impossible for reasons of practicality or otherwise.

In the case of databases, the requirement that the source is indicated is likely to be met by citing the database and not the individual works within the database, if this is impossible for reasons of practicality.

New automated textual analysis techniques work by the bulk copying of electronic information which is analysed for patterns, trends and other useful information. The analytical technologies used involve acts of copying, even where the products of those technologies do not contain protectable expressions or affect the markets for the primary works.

Copying in this way without the permission of the rights holders would previously have risked infringing copyright. Before the introduction of the data mining exception it meant that research was being hampered because, for example, academics wishing to undertake textual analysis across a large number of journal articles from a wide variety of publishers would have needed to seek the permission of each of those publishers one by one. However, the exception inserted into section 29A of the CDPA by SI 2014/1372 now allows computer-based analysis (known as text and data mining) of copyright material to be undertaken for non-commercial research without having to obtain specific permission from the rights holder.

The whole point of data mining is that it is a technique which works best when the textual analysis is applied across large quantities of content. Inevitably if you have to get permission from individual publishers the whole process can be time-consuming, and there is absolutely no guarantee that each of the publishers would permit the use of data mining techniques to be used on their content. Some might not respond at all to permission requests, others may take a while to respond, and yet others may wish to impose a fee for the privilege of doing data analytics.

Putting an exception into law overcomes these difficulties, but only up to a point. If vendors impose technical barriers that prevent you from being able to benefit from the data mining exception you will need to approach them directly to see if an amicable solution can be found. And if that fails you would be able to make a formal complaint to the Secretary of State for Business Innovation and Skills about the publishers' use of technological protection measures. There is a complaints form available from the Intellectual Property Office website for this purpose. But all of this raises the question of how long the process would take, and whether the moment of need to undertake data analytics has long since passed by the time a response to the complaint is received.

The ability of researchers to copy materials for the technical process of text and data mining is qualified by the need for them to have lawful access to the works in question. This term 'lawful access' would cover both paid-for subscribed content, as well as content that is not paid for but where, for example, there is a right of access under a licence such as a Creative Commons licence. Where a person has lawful access to read any copyright material, because of the section 29A exception they do not have to obtain additional permission from rights holders in order to copy the work for text and data mining for non-commercial research. The exception does not, however, provide a 'right to data mine' works to which the researcher does not already have a right of access. Researchers or their institutions will still have to buy access to content if that is the rights holder's business model.

The impact assessment[5] says 'It will not prevent the publisher/provider from applying technical protection measures on networks used in order to maintain security or stability. It will not prevent the publisher/provider from offering licensed services, or from licensing all commercial activities in this area.'

At the time of the consultation process[6] some publishers and their representatives expressed concern over the possibility that their systems could be overloaded with an influx of requests, and the provision for data mining clearly takes this into account. In *Exceptions to Copyright: research* (guidance from the IPO, 2014) it says:

> Publishers can apply technological measures on networks that are required in order to maintain security or stability but won't be able to enforce contract terms that seek to prevent or unreasonably restrict text and data mining. Controls could include imposing reasonable limits on download speeds. These controls should not stop researchers from benefiting from the exception.

The data mining exception includes a clause which prevents publishers from being able to use contract override in order to get out of the user's right to mine the data to which they have lawful access.

3.6.4   Making of temporary copies (s 28A)

Article 5 of the Copyright Directive (2001/29/EC) contains only one compulsory exception which all member states must have in their national legislation, and that is the exception relating to the making of temporary or transient copies. All of the other exceptions contained in Article 5 are, in effect, a picklist from which member states can select those exceptions that they wish to have in their copyright laws. Recital 33 of the Copyright Directive tells us the intention behind the compulsory exception:

> The exclusive right of reproduction should be subject to an exception to allow certain acts of temporary reproduction, which are transient or incidental reproductions, forming an integral and essential part of a technological process and carried out for the sole purpose of enabling either efficient transmission in a network between third parties by an intermediary, or a lawful use of a work or other subject-matter to be made. The acts of reproduction concerned should have no separate economic value on their own. To the extent that they meet these conditions, this exception should include acts which enable browsing as well as acts of caching to take place, including those which enable transmission systems to function efficiently, provided that the intermediary does not modify the information and does not interfere with the lawful use of technology, widely recognised and used by industry, to obtain data on the use of the information. A use should be considered lawful where it is authorised by the rightholder or not restricted by law.

The exception was implemented in the UK as section 28A of the CDPA 1988. It states that:

> Copyright in a literary work, other than a computer program or a database, or in a dramatic, musical or artistic work, the typographical arrangement of a published edition, a sound recording or a film, is not infringed by the making of a temporary copy which is transient or incidental, which is an integral and essential part of a technological process and the sole purpose of which is to enable (a) a transmission of the work in a network between third parties by an intermediary; or (b) a lawful use of the work; and which has no independent economic significance.
>
> Source: The National Archives, 2015

So, in order to qualify for the exception the following conditions need to be met:

- The copy made must be transient or incidental.
- It should be an integral and essential part of a technological process.
- The sole purpose of the copy being made is to transmit the work between third parties by an intermediary OR to enable a lawful use of the work.
- It should have no independent economic significance.

The concept of what is 'transient' was explored in Infopaq International AS v Danske Dagblades Forening (C-5/08).

Infopaq International AS v Danske Dagblades Forening (C-5/08)

The European Court of Justice found that the act of printing out an extract of 11 words, during a data capture process such as that at issue in the Infopaq proceedings, does not fulfil the condition of being transient in nature as required by Article 5(1) of Directive 2001/29 and, therefore, that process cannot be carried out without the consent of the relevant rights holders.

Infopaq printed out the 11-word extracts, and as such it would require human intervention for the print-outs to be destroyed. The exception in Article 5, and which the UK has implemented through section 28A, only covers copies that are made as an integral part of a technological process where they are automatically deleted at the end of that process. So, the duration of the act of copying must be limited to what is necessary for the proper completion of the technological process in question.

The case of Public Relations Consultants Association Limited (PRCA) (Appellant) v The Newspaper Licensing Agency Limited (NLA) and others (Respondents) is a landmark case which considered the meaning of the section 28A exception on the making of copies which are temporary or transient.

PRCA v NLA (commonly known as the Meltwater case)[7]

The case commonly known as the Meltwater case (which appears as either PRCA v NLA or NLA v Meltwater Holding, depending on which stage it had reached) went to the High Court ([2010] EWHC 3099 (Ch), the Court of Appeal ([2011] EWCA Civ 890), the Supreme Court ([2013] UKSC 18), and ultimately to the European Court of Justice (case C-360/13). The CJEU's ruling was crucial, because had they reached a different conclusion, it would have meant that when citizens browsed websites, such as those belonging to newspaper publishers, they would be infringing copyright law on a daily basis.

Background: Meltwater provides an online media monitoring service called Meltwater News. Subscribers to the service are sent e-mails containing the headlines of online articles, hyperlinks to the articles on publishers' websites and short extracts of the articles themselves. The NLA brought proceedings for copyright infringement against Meltwater and PRCA. The NLA claimed that end-users of Meltwater News required a licence to receive it because, through their ordinary use of the service, on-screen and cached copies of copyright-protected works would be made on the end-users' computers when they accessed and browsed newspaper websites.

Both the High Court and the Court of Appeal held that end-users of Meltwater News needed a licence from the NLA and that they could not rely on the temporary copies exception.

The Supreme Court noted that the e-mail copy is not temporary, because it is stored on the recipient's hard drive until the end-user chooses to delete it; but they ruled that the temporary copies exception should apply to on-screen and 'cached' copies of copyright-protected works which are generated in the course of ordinary internet browsing.

The Supreme Court referred the case to the European Court of Justice to clarify the meaning of the temporary copies exception, because the points at issue were significant and it was important to get a CJEU ruling as this would apply uniformly across the European Union.

The CJEU found that Article 5 of Directive 2001/29/EC must be interpreted as meaning that the copies on the user's computer screen and the copies in the internet 'cache' of that computer's hard disk, made by an end-user in the course of viewing a website, satisfy the conditions that those copies must be temporary, transient or incidental in nature and that they constituted an integral and essential part of a technological process.

3.6.5   Disabled persons – making accessible copies (ss 31A–31F)

The Copyright and Rights in Performances (Disability) Regulations 2014 (SI 2014/1384) introduced three exceptions relating to copying for disabled persons. Section 31A covers the making of copies of works for personal use either by a disabled person, or a person acting on behalf of the disabled person; section 31B covers the making and supply of accessible copies by authorized bodies for the personal use of disabled persons; and section 31BA permits the making of intermediate copies where this is necessary in order to make an accessible copy.

There are a series of provisions relating to the record-keeping and notification requirements with regard to the making of accessible and intermediate copies by authorized bodies (section 31BB). It is also worth pointing out that institutions must continue to keep records for copies made under the previous exceptions (31B and C).

Section 31F contains definitions of 'disabled person', 'accessible copy' and 'authorized body'.

The term **'disabled person'** is defined as 'a person who has a physical or mental impairment which prevents the person from enjoying a copyright work to the same degree as a person who does not have that impairment' (see 31F (2)) (Source: IPO, 2014).

The term **'accessible copy'** means a version of a copyright work which enables the fuller enjoyment of the work by disabled persons. The accessible copy may include facilities for navigating around the version of the work, but what would not be permitted under the disability exception in section 31 of the CDPA 1988 is the inclusion of any changes to the work which are not necessary to overcome the problems suffered by the disabled persons for whom the accessible copy is intended.

According to section 31F(6) **'authorised body'** means (a) an educational establishment, or (b) a body that is not conducted for profit (Source: The National Archives, 2015).

Some respondents to the IPO's consultation process suggested changing the definition of disability from 'physical or mental impairment' to 'physical, cognitive or mental impairment'. This is because dyslexia is considered by some people to be a cognitive rather than a mental impairment. However, the government decided to retain the original definition, as this correlates with the definition used in the Equality Act 2010. In fact, the British Dyslexia Association notes on its website that dyslexia falls within the definition provided in the Equality Act.

If any type of copyright work is not available commercially in a format that can be accessed by a disabled person, an individual, educational establishment or charity is able to make an accessible copy for them.

The Copyright, Designs and Patents Act 1988 as amended by the Copyright (Visually Impaired Persons) Act 2002 previously allowed individuals and charities to make copies of books in accessible formats for blind and visually impaired people. This meant that, where a book was unavailable in an accessible format such as Braille, audio or large print, an accessible copy could be made and provided to a visually impaired person without infringing copyright. The 2002 Act was repealed by The Copyright and Rights in Performances (Disability) Regulations 2014: SI 2014/1384, which broadened the exceptions in the CDPA 1988 to cover disabilities more widely.

The Copyright, Designs and Patents Act 1988 previously contained provisions allowing organizations to create subtitled copies of broadcasts for people who are deaf or hard of hearing, as long as the organization had been designated to do so by the Secretary of State. The changes to the law brought about in 2014 by SI 2014/1384 mean that organizations wishing to produce subtitled copies of broadcasts on behalf of deaf and other disabled people are now able to do so without going through a bureaucratic designation process.

The Copyright and Rights in Performances (Disability) Regulations 2014 (SI

2014/1384) extended the scope of the law in this area. As a result it is now possible to copy any type of copyright work for the benefit of people with any (physical or mental) impairment, if and to the extent that the impairment prevents them from accessing a copyright work. As already noted, they also simplify the law by removing the designation process for organizations that create subtitled copies of broadcasts.

Where an institution makes an accessible copy for a disabled person, it needs to bear in mind the following point if the work is copy-protected:

> If an accessible copy is made under this section of a work which is in copy-protected
> electronic form, the accessible copy must, so far as is reasonably practicable,
> incorporate the same or equally effective copy protection (unless the copyright owner
> agrees otherwise).   CDPA 1988 s 31B(8). Source: IPO, 2014

So, for example, if an accessible copy of a copy-protected PDF is made, then it must have the protection reinstated once the necessary copying has been done. There is no requirement for creators to remove the protection measure and it is still technically illegal to circumvent it.

The Regulations state that

> An authorised body which has made an accessible copy of a work under this section
> may supply it to another authorised body which is entitled to make accessible copies of
> the work under this section for the purposes of enabling that other body to make
> accessible copies of the work
>
> CDPA 1988 s 31B(9) Source: The National Archives, 2015

The UK has signed the Marrakesh Treaty. If and when the UK ratifies the Treaty, there will then be a cross-border dimension to the making of copies for disabled persons. Under the Treaty authorized entities are able to perform cross-border exchanges, although these authorized entities do have a number of duties and responsibilities placed upon them (for further details see Section 2.1.5 above).

3.6.6   Personal copies for private use (s 28B)

NB This exception has been quashed following a judicial review challenge brought by organizations representing the music industry. For further information see [2015] EWHC 1723 (Admin) and [2015] EWHC 2041 (Admin).

See: www.bailii.org/ew/cases/EWHC/Admin/2015/1723.html and www.bailii.org/ew/cases/EWHC/Admin/2015/2041.html for details.

Notes

1   Berne Convention for the protection of literary and artistic works, Article 9:
    'Right of reproduction'.
2   Hargreaves, Ian (2011) *Digital Opportunity: a review of intellectual property and
    growth*, www.gov.uk/government/publications/digital-opportunity-review-of-
    intellectual-property-and-growth.
3   International Association of Scientific, Technical and Medical Publishers
    (2008) *Guidelines For Quotation And Other Academic Uses Of Excerpts From
    Journal Articles*, http://ocw.kyoto-u.ac.jp/en/copyright-en/files/11Elsevier.pdf.
4   References to a librarian or archivist include a person acting on behalf of a
    librarian or archivist.
5   https://www.gov.uk/government/uploads/system/uploads/attachment_
    data/file/308738/ia-exception-dataanalytics.pdf.
6   The IPO's 'Consultation on copyright' ran for 14 weeks from 14 December
    2011 through to 21 March 2012.
7   The Meltwater case went through the High Court, Court of Appeal and the
    Supreme Court, as well as the CJEU. The names of the parties changed
    during that process, and the case references for the various stages are: PRCA
    v NLA C-360/13, [2013] UKSC 18; NLA v Meltwater Holding [2011]
    EWCA Civ 890, [2010] EWHC 3099 (Ch).
8   http://curia.europa.eu/juris/document/document.jsf?text=&docid=
    131555&pageIndex=0&doclang=en&mode=lst&dir=&occ=first&part=1&ci
    d=447274.
9   www.gov.uk/government/publications/technological-protection-measures-
    tpms-complaints-process.

Licensing

Chapter 4 covers:

See also Section 6.2.2 on p. 137 on orphan works licences.

4.1   Introduction to licensing

A licence gives permission to do something that, without there being a licence in place, would be an infringement of copyright. For example, a non-exclusive licence to use an e-book service gives the subscriber limited rights to use the service, and it enables the licensor to retain the right to license the service to other people. The wording of the agreement will typically set out the uses that are permitted under the licence as well as a series of limitations to those permitted uses. One example of how the permitted uses could be limited would be where the agreement wording expressly forbids the subscriber from being able to sell, licence, sublicense, or distribute the content to third parties.

Copyright law limits the copying of protected works, and entering into a license agreement is a way of being able to get more rights, allowing you to carry out a wider range of copying activities than would otherwise have been the case. Where your copying is not covered by one of the copyright exceptions, a licence may provide the answer. The licence will provide a lawful solution to the copying. Often people will pay for the privilege of entering into such a licence agreement. But that is not always the case. For example, the Creative Commons licences, the Open Government Licence and the Open Parliament Licence are all available free of charge.

Licensing can be a significant source of income for companies and institutions that are copyright owners.

Licences can result from negotiations between the person granting the licence, who is known as the licensor, and the person receiving the licence, who is known as the licensee, although not all licences are negotiated (see Section 4.2.2 below).

Licences could be issued directly by the rights holder, or through someone who has been given the authority by the rights holder to act on their behalf. For example, there are a number of agencies such as the Copyright Licensing Agency or the Music Publishers Association[1] that act on behalf of rights owners and these agencies issue licences permitting copying which would not otherwise be allowed.

4.2   The different types of licence
4.2.1   Exclusive and non-exclusive licences

The sorts of licence that information professionals normally encounter are *non-exclusive* – in other words, the intellectual property owner may use and license the content to more than one licensee. By way of example, imagine a licence agreement for the use of an online database. It will usually be a product that is available to anyone who is able to pay the subscription fee and who accepts the terms of the licence agreement.

The opposite of a non-exclusive licence is for the licensor and licensee to enter into an *exclusive* licence agreement. In that scenario the licensee is the only person who can use the intellectual property, and the licensor is not entitled to use the intellectual property themselves.

4.2.2   Licences which aren't negotiated

There are a number of different types of licence in which negotiation doesn't play a part:

* Shrink wrap licence. When you buy a piece of off-the-shelf software it is likely to be governed by a 'shrink wrap' agreement. The term 'shrink wrap' refers to the way in which some of the key terms of the agreement are visible underneath the cellophane wrapping, and the moment you tear open the wrapping you are deemed to have accepted the terms of the agreement.

- Click-use licence. This is where you simply have a choice as to whether to accept the terms of use for an online work as they stand, or to reject them. In some instances the 'I accept' button is greyed out until the user has navigated through the wording of the licence terms.
- Browse wrap licence. This is where the terms and conditions of use of a website or service are available on the site and can be accessed using a hyperlink, but unlike a click-use, or a click-wrap, agreement the user isn't forced to read the terms before being able to access the service.

There is a useful publication from the Electronic Frontier Foundation[2] which ✱ looks at the various ways in which a web user might agree to an online set of terms and conditions.

4.2.3 Licences which are negotiated

Where a licence for an electronic product is negotiable, clearly the price paid for the subscription is a key area of negotiation. But other aspects of the licence are just as important. For example, the definition of the terms 'permitted users', 'authorized uses' and 'site' can make a big difference with regard to what you are paying for. The definitions of those terms will determine how many people are able to access the service and what they are allowed to do with the content, and will also determine whether 'site' is referred to as a physical location or whether it is interpreted in a more flexible way – such as, for example, where it relates to anyone who has access to a secure electronic network. If the licence is based on there being a single simultaneous user, for example, that could potentially be anyone working for the organization regardless of which office they are based in or indeed of which country they are based in, provided that only one person at a time is signed into the service. Indeed, in an academic setting this has always been a big issue because it potentially restricts access to core reading. From a publisher's point of view, the question of how many users can access content simultaneously goes to the very heart of their business model, and any relaxation on this point may be dependent upon the price charged for the service. Other issues that also need to be considered include:

- Can authorized users make copies?
- Can they redistribute copies?
- Can they translate or make an adaptation of copies?

4.3   The relationship between contracts/licences and copyright

It is essential to understand the interrelationship between copyright and contract law, because there are some instances whereby copyright exceptions can be overridden by contracts or licence agreements and other instances where that is expressly forbidden.

Exceptions which can be overridden by contracts include the exception in section 40B of CDPA 1988, which covers libraries and educational establishments, etc.: making works available through dedicated terminals. Under this exception the work must be communicated or made available in compliance with any purchase or licensing terms to which it is subject.

There are a number of copyright exceptions which cannot be overridden by contracts. They include the exceptions for non-commercial research (section 29), private study (section 29), quotation (section 30), parody (section 30A), text and data mining (section 29A) and copying by librarians – single copies of published works (section 42A).

For an exception not to be overridden by contracts or licences, the wording of that exception would need to explicitly say so. For example, the exception for quotation (section 30(1ZA) of the CDPA 1988) says:

> to the extent that a term of a contract purports to prevent or restrict the doing of any act which, by virtue of subsection (1ZA), would not infringe copyright, that term is unenforceable.
>
> Source: IPO, 2014

The reason that you need to look out for wording along these lines is that UK copyright law does not have a general provision treating all of the exceptions as rights which cannot be overridden by contract law. In contrast to the UK approach, the copyright laws of countries like Portugal, Ireland and Belgium make the exceptions imperative, where they cannot be overridden by contract.

Some contracts have a clause reaffirming statutory rights. For example, a licence agreement might have a form of words along the following lines:

> This agreement is without prejudice to any acts which the licensee is permitted to carry out by the terms of the Copyright, Designs and Patents Act 1988, and nothing herein shall be construed as affecting or diminishing such permitted acts in any way whatsoever.

Or another example form of words could be:

> This Licence shall be deemed to complement and extend the rights of the Institution and Authorised Users under the Copyright, Designs and Patents Act 1988 and nothing

in this Licence shall constitute a waiver of any statutory rights held by the Institution and Authorised Users from time to time under the Act or any amending legislation.

The IPO's guidance published in March 2014, entitled *Exceptions to Copyright: libraries, archives and museums*, addresses the question of the impact of the legislative changes on contracts which were signed before the changes to the copyright exceptions took effect:

> "I have a licence granted under the old law, what happens once the new law comes in?"

> If your licence grants wider permissions than the new law, then your licence will be unaffected. If the new law lets you do more than your licence, then you can rely on the new law. Your licence will still be valid, but in so far as any term says you cannot do something allowed by the new law, you will not have to comply with that term.

For further information, see Kretschmer, Martin et al. (2010) *The Relationship Between Copyright and Contract Law*, SABIP. See also the tables in Chapter 3 above: Table 3.1, Copyright exceptions that cannot be overridden by contracts (p. 38), and Table 3.2, The interface between exceptions and licences (pp. 38–9).

4.4   Negotiating licences

Licences are often – but not always – open to negotiation, and I am thinking here not just of negotiation around price, but also concerning other licence terms, such as the permitted uses that can be made of the content, who are deemed to be authorized users, and how many people that covers. There are, however, a number of licences which are presented without any opportunity for negotiation. They include shrink wrap agreements, Creative Commons licences and terms and conditions which appear on websites (see also Section 4.2.2 above).

4.4.1   Negotiating copyright clearance for a particular work

One type of licence which can be open to negotiation is the licence for using third-party content in something you publish. An important aspect of the agreement is that it will set out the agreed copyright clearance fee. It could be thought of as a publishing permit. In an article by Melanie Newman in the *THE*[3] it is clear that these licence fees are negotiable. It doesn't for one moment mean that it would be easy to negotiate the level of the fee, or indeed to negotiate over whether a fee is going to be levied at all. But it is certainly worth asking for a reduction in the level of the fee that is initially proposed. The article tells how a retired professor had hit out at the copyright clearance charges which he had initially been presented with when writing a textbook. The projected royalties from his book were £3000 based on 1000 sales. Unless all of the copies of the book were sold within the first year, that figure of £3000 would be spread over a number of years; and if it were based on net receipts, the figure could potentially be far less if the publisher gave some of the copies away as review copies and sold some of the copies at a discount. The article mentions seven items which required clearance, where the initial clearance fees would have added up to well over a third of the maximum potential royalties. After some haggling, one of the clearance costs was waived altogether while another was revised down to a quarter of the amount that was initially quoted.

4.4.2 Negotiating licences for access to and use of electronic products

Another type of licence which is open to negotiation is the licence for access to and use of electronic products. The outcome of those negotiations will in part depend upon the relative bargaining power of both sides as well as the negotiating skills of each party. But there are a number of things which will help the licensee to ensure that the negotiations are as effective as they can possibly be:

- Start the process well ahead of the renewal date.
- Gather together relevant background information:
  - reliability and performance of the product
  - the main users of the product
  - the value of this product to your organization (low, medium, high)
  - usage data: is the usage going up or down, or is it quite stable? If the product is based on the number of simultaneous users, how often are people turned away because of the limit having been reached?
  - any other dealings your organization has with the vendor (for example, does another part of the organization subscribe to the same product, or to a different one from the same provider?)
- Do some research on any alternatives that are on the market.
  - Would they really be an adequate alternative?
  - How much do they cost?
  - Do they have the level of functionality that you need?
- Are there any modules you no longer need or that you would like to add to your subscription?
- Make sure that only the necessary people are involved.
- Keep detailed records (look at your notes from last year's negotiations – were there any issues that you didn't get time to follow up on?).
- If you are not happy with elements of the licence, tell the supplier.
- Remember that the negotiation isn't just about price.
- Make sure that you have key documents to hand, such as:

— a set of licensing principles which could be used as a checklist (see, for example, the IFLA licensing principles, www.ifla.org/publications/ifla-licensing-principles-2001)
— a model licence agreement such as the ones available from JISC Collections, www.jisc-collections.ac.uk/model_licence
— a grid or table setting out the minimum requirements you want your licences to include.

Prior to the negotiations, clarify what your requirements are:

- Are there any forthcoming planned developments which could impact the need for the product?
- Is your organization required to tender for contracts above a certain value?
- What access is required?
- Do you need to send the information to clients?
- Do you want the right to republish extracts?
- Are there any advantages to having an extended subscription?
- What is the budget? (It is best to avoid revealing the budget to the supplier, but knowing the maximum available budget will help you during the negotiation process – it could, for example, be that you conclude that the price being offered to you is so far away from the amount your organization is willing to pay that there seems little point in negotiating any further.)

4.5   The rationale for collective licences

Copyright clearance can be a time-consuming process both for the copyright owner and for the user of copyright-protected content. Collective licensing can be a win-win for both sides because it provides a simple and cost-effective solution, both for those who wish to copy from published materials without breaking the law, and for rights holders, for whom it provides a way of dealing with second rights without the need for direct licensing, which would be inefficient and costly for the amount of money that it would raise.

Rights owners such as authors, publishers, and visual artists can mandate a collective licensing society to act on their behalf. Rather than having to build up for themselves an expertise in second rights, having to negotiate agreements directly with users, to raise invoices and so on, they can instead opt to mandate a collecting society to act on their behalf.

Users of copyright material can benefit from the licences offered by the collecting societies. The availability of blanket licences allows users to copy from a repertoire of content from a wide range of rights owners in return for a single licence fee, which is much more efficient than having to deal with lots of right holders individually. It makes it much more efficient in terms of time, the administration involved, and in terms of cost. The fee that the user pays for the licence is then distributed amongst the rights holders whose works have been copied (such as publishers, authors or visual artists), after the collecting societies' operating costs have been taken into account.

PwC[4] say that there is an economic rationale for collective licensing through collective management organizations (CMOs) because they are able to achieve economies of scale which help to minimize the transaction costs associated with rights management. They take the example of the higher education sector as a case study and estimate that transaction costs for users and rights owners through CMOs are around £6.7 million a year; whereas this would be between £145 and £720 million a year if the higher education sector were relying on an atomized model – by which they mean where the institutions would have had to deal directly with individual publishers.

4.6   Collective licensing societies
4.6.1   Copyright Licensing Agency

The Copyright Licensing Agency (CLA) issue licences to organizations that wish to copy and re-use published works. This includes the photocopying, scanning, and re-use of content from magazines, books, journals and online publications, as well as press cuttings or documents supplied by a licensed third party.

CLA licences permit copying from most titles published within the UK and over 30 international territories. The money raised from issuing licences is distributed to authors, publishers and visual artists.

CLA offer a wide range of licences, and so it is necessary to refer to the terms of the specific licence that applies to your sector. They include:

- standard CLA business licence
- multinational business licence
- licences for educational establishments
  — schools
  — further education
  — higher education
- licence for pharmaceutical companies
- licence for law firms
- licence for PR and media agencies
- licence for media monitoring organizations
- licence for hotels and conference centres
- NHS licence
- central government licence
- public administration licence (for other public sector organizations)

- website republishing licence
- document delivery licence
- print disability licence
- library licence scheme (to cover walk-in users making copies for commercial purposes).

The CLA has a number of different licences which are geared to a number of different sectors, and so it is impossible – indeed dangerous – to give general statements, as though they apply across all of the licences. To illustrate how the licences work, I have taken the example of the standard business licence, but if your organization operates under a different CLA licence, you will need to look at its terms and conditions.

4.6.1.1   Amount limits

Each licence sets out a series of amount limits. It is important to note that these differ between licences. In the case of the standard business licence:

> No Licensed Copy shall exceed the greater of 5% of any item of Licensed Material, or:
> — In the case of a periodical publication, one whole article; or
> — In the case of a published report of judicial proceedings, the entire report of a single case; or
> — In the case of a book, one chapter.
>
> Source: CLA standard business licence clause 4.2,
> www.cla.co.uk/data/pdfs/business/businesslicence_sep2011.pdf

4.6.1.2   Excluded works and categories

Each licence has a set of excluded categories and works which are not covered by the licence, and so it is important to check the list that applies to your sector (www.cla.co.uk/licences/excluded_works). The excluded categories which apply to the business and the public sector are:

- printed music (including the words)
- maps and charts
- newspapers
- workbooks, workcards or assignment sheets
- any work on which the copyright owner has expressly and prominently stipulated that it may not be copied under a CLA licence.

In addition to the list of excluded categories, there is a list of excluded works. Some entries will specify that all publications from a particular publisher cannot be copied under the licence; whilst many other entries will specify particular titles which cannot be copied.

There is a title search facility to check permissions: www.cla.co.uk/licences/titlesearch. It helps licensees to be able to quickly see what can be copied, shared or re-used legally with a CLA licence. There is also a CLA title search app, www.cla.co.uk/licences/checkpermissions/mobileapp, where you can use your phone to read the ISBN or ISSN barcode on a publication, and quickly retrieve the information for a specific title. When looking up a title, you have to specify which type of licence you hold. Rights holders can choose whether they wish their titles to be covered by the CLA's licences, and they can specify for which types of licence they are giving a mandate. The aim of the title search facility and the app version is to try and simplify as much as possible the whole process.

'What can I do with this content' (www.whatcanidowiththiscontent.com) is a copyright icon which is used to display a publisher's copyright terms to viewers of their website or online publication. It indicates that the content is protected by copyright; it tells end-users that the publisher's content is covered by the CLA's licences; and it displays the terms in a clear and simple summary to reflect the publisher's terms – whether it can be printed, whether extracts can be used in other materials, whether it can be shared on an intranet and whether it can be shared externally.

Most of the CLA's licence fees are charged on the basis of staff numbers in the licensee's organization. In the case of the business licence it is based on the number of professional employees. In the case of the higher education licence, the fees are calculated based on the number of full-time equivalent students. As the fee for the standard business licence is based on the number of professional employees, it is obviously important to be clear about how these are to be counted. By way of example, the number of professional employees for the standard business licence is calculated by counting employees, contracted workers or consultants who are either managers and senior officials; professional occupations; or associate professional and technical occupations (based on the Office for National Statistics occupational classifications). See www.cla.co.uk/licences/licences_available/business/licence_fee.

4.6.2   NLA Media Access

NLA Media Access is a publisher-owned rights licensing and database company founded in 1996. It provides access to and licenses the re-use of published content in the media monitoring market. Licences available include:

- business licence
- public relations licence
- charity licence

- higher education licence
- corporate website republishing licence
- web end-user licence.

Originally known as the Newspaper Licensing Agency, the company used to licence the use of UK national and regional newspapers, as well as some foreign newspapers. These days NLA Media Access has licences which authorize users to copy from a range of newspapers, magazines and websites.

In 2013 the Professional Publishers Association recommended the NLA Media Access licensing model to its members, and over 150 publishers opted for their content to be licensed through the NLA. Many titles which were once covered by the Copyright Licensing Agency are now covered instead by NLA Media Access. Depending upon the titles that are copied, this change does mean that some organizations may need to consider having licences from both the CLA and the NLA to cover the copying of magazines.

NLA Media Access also provides database services both to media monitoring agencies and also to publishers:

- eClips – there are a number of sites that fall under the heading of 'eClips', such as www.clipsearch.co.uk and www.newspapersforschools.co.uk
  — ClipSearch is a database with content from over 100 UK national and regional newspapers which can be used to research the news and to find original articles
  — ClipShare is a service used by around 7000 UK journalists. The database holds over 55 million individual articles. It covers web as well as print content back to 2001.
- PhotoChecker provides photo libraries with a way of being able to track the use of publications in the eClips database, to enable contracts to be monitored and to facilitate prompt payment
- NLA Media Access operates an Online Article Tracking Service (http://oats.nla.co.uk) which identifies where content taken from national newspaper websites has been copied elsewhere in the public domain, and the service is being extended to a wider range of publishers.

In 2013 NLA Media Access announced that it had entered into a partnership with the Copyright Licensing Agency for the latter to act as the NLA's agent for the licensing of newspaper publications in the education sector. This applies to UK schools and to the higher education sector. The rationale was that by providing a single point of contact and centralized administration it would simplify copyright licensing in the education sector.

4.6.3 Design and Artists Copyright Society

The Design and Artists Copyright Society (DACS, www.dacs.org.uk) is a rights management organization which represents visual artists such as:

* painters
* sculptors
* photographers
* cartoonists
* illustrators
* craftspersons
* designers
* digital artists.

DACS runs a copyright licensing service for British and international customers who want to be able to reproduce works by the artists it represents. The royalties are paid to artists and their estates four times a year.

Payback is an annual scheme which pays royalties to visual artists and estates whose work has been reproduced in UK books, magazines or on television. These royalties come from collective licensing schemes. Payback is open to all kinds of visual artists and also to artists' estates and their representatives.

Artist's Resale Right: Under directive 2001/84/EC artists and their heirs are entitled to a royalty where their work is resold for€€1000 or more by an art market professional. DACS operates an artist's resale right service whereby if a royalty is generated by a resale of a work by one of its members, DACS will collect the royalty and pay it to the member.

In 2014 DACS launched **Artimage** (www.dacs.org.uk/licensing-works/ artimage), a digital image resource which showcases and licenses exceptional works of modern and contemporary art. DACS provides the licence agreement and image file, and thereby creates a streamlined process for publishing, merchandizing and advertising needs. The fees collected go back to support artists and their estates.

4.6.4 Educational Recording Agency

The Educational Recording Agency (ERA) operates on behalf of its members a licensing scheme for the educational use of broadcast material both in the classroom and by students at home. There are currently 20 members of ERA (see Figure 4.1), representing broadcasters, writers, visual creators, composers, directors and performers. The ERA licensing scheme permits the staff of educational establishments to record, for non-commercial educational purposes, from the broadcast output of the ERA's members. The ERA licence enables educational establishments to create libraries or repositories of broadcasts which can be used for teaching and learning.

> Association De Gestion Internationale Collective Des Oeuvres Audiovisuelles
> Authors' Licensing and Collecting Society Limited
> BBC Worldwide Limited
> BPI (British Recorded Music Industry) Limited
> Channel Four Television Corporation
> Channel 5 Broadcasting Limited
> Compact Collections Limited (acting as agent for Discovery, National Geographic Channel and AETN UK)
> Design and Artists Copyright Society
> Directors UK Limited
> Equity
> Focal International Limited
> The Incorporated Society of Musicians
> ITV Network Limited
> Mechanical-Copyright Protection Society Limited (MCPS)
> Musicians' Union
> Open University Worldwide Limited
> The Performing Right Society Limited
> Phonographic Performance Limited
> Radio Independents Group
> Sianel Pedwar Cymru (S4C)

Figure 4.1 *ERA members (for an up-to-date list check www.era.org.uk)*

The ERA licence covers recording from all scheduled free-to-air radio and television broadcasts. It also covers the accessing and downloading of content from 'on-demand' services such as the BBC's iPlayer, 4oD, or Demand5. The CDPA 1988 doesn't consider on-demand services to fall within the definition of a 'broadcast', but the ERA licence is able to cover them as a result of changes that were made to the terms and conditions of its broadcaster members.

The ERA licence does not cover:

- showing recordings for entertainment purposes
- the inclusion of recordings or extracts within any corporate materials to promote the educational establishment
- the use of stills from recordings on the educational establishment's website
- sale or commercial hire of recordings
- materials directly accessed from YouTube, whose terms and conditions require that the material is for 'personal use only'
- advertisements, because ERA members do not own or control the rights in them.

ERA cannot license public libraries, commercial training organizations or the educational units of museums and galleries, because these do not fall within the definition of 'educational establishment' for the purposes of the CDPA 1988. (The details of what constitutes an 'educational establishment' for the purposes of the Copyright, Designs and Patents Act 1988 can be found in The Copyright (Educational Establishments) Order: SI 2005/223.)

The ERA licence would cover online relay to registered students both on and off site, where this is done using whiteboards and virtual learning environments. The ERA licence would also cover the recording of extracts of programmes, as well as the recording of an entire programme. However, it would not cover the adaptation of broadcasts, nor the amendment, distortion or mutilation of material. Instead, programme material must be used as broadcast. Programme credits should not be edited from broadcasts.

Recordings made after 30 May 1990[5] can be held indefinitely if there is a continuing need for them, provided the educational establishment continues to hold a valid ERA licence. However, recordings which are no longer needed must be destroyed. They can't be sold or otherwise dealt with.

All recordings need to be labelled with the following information:

- date (when the recording was made)
- name of the broadcaster
- programme title
- the wording 'This recording is to be used only for educational and non-commercial purposes under the terms of the ERA licence'.

ERA sells sheets of labels for this purpose; alternatively, licensees can ask for a template for the labels for A4 laser printing.

Supplying recordings to distance learners outside the UK, whether that be in hard copy or by electronic means, is not permitted under the terms of ERA's licence. In theory, the ability to give students overseas access to a recording could be overcome through the use of a licence. However, as noted above, at present ERA's licence does not permit overseas access to content, regardless of any measures that might be put in place to limit access to an educational establishment's pupils and staff (such as the use of authentication).

4.6.5   Maps: copying and lending

4.6.5.1   Ordnance Survey[6]

Ordnance Survey (OS) maps which are less than 50 years old are subject to Crown copyright. This means that copying an Ordnance Survey map (for example, photocopying, scanning, tracing or printing electronic data) is likely to be an infringement of Crown copyright unless such copying falls within the exceptions permitted by the Copyright, Designs and Patents Act 1988.

Ordnance Survey offers a range of licences and agreements:

- OS OpenData
- OS OpenSpace API

- derived data and free to use terms
- framework contract for direct customers
- framework contract for partners
- framework trade agreement
- multi-client contractor licence
- addressing multi-contractor agreement for the public sector
- data management licensing services
- paper map copying licence
- copying paper mapping in libraries and archives
- publishing licence
- innovation licence
- licensing for education
- media licence.

Ordnance Survey offer a dozen products which are available free of charge as open data.[7]

LACA agreement with Ordnance Survey

The Libraries and Archives Copyright Alliance (LACA) is a UK umbrella group convened by CILIP, the Chartered Institute of Library and Information Professionals. LACA brings together the UK's major professional organizations and experts representing librarians and archivists to lobby in the UK and Europe about copyright issues which impact delivery of access to knowledge and information by libraries, archives and information services in the digital age.

Prior to June 2014 librarians were not able under section 39 of the CDPA 1988 to copy maps on behalf of their users. This was because maps are treated as artistic works and section 39 did not cover the copying of artistic works by librarians for their users. As a result, it was necessary for LACA to negotiate an agreement with Ordnance Survey in 2006.[8] The agreement regularized and clarified the conditions under which librarians and archivists were able to copy mapping for users. Under the 2006 LACA/Ordnance Survey agreement:

- Librarians and archivists within 'prescribed libraries and archives' were formally permitted to copy from OS copyright paper and electronic mapping for users without having specific licensing in place.
- OS did not object to up to four copies of no more than 625 sq. cm being made from paper maps or the production of prints from electronic data by librarians and archivists, provided that the prescribed conditions set out in section 39(2) of the Act were complied with.
- OS required that each copy made was accompanied by an acknowledgement (unless this was impossible for reasons of practicality or otherwise) in the

following form: © Crown Copyright. Reproduced by permission of Ordnance Survey®.

However, it should be pointed out that the agreement was drafted in 2006, and that there have been a number of changes to copyright law since then which are relevant to the copying of maps. These include the following:

- Librarians are now able to copy maps on behalf of their users under section 42A (which replaced the old section 39), and the wording of the new section doesn't distinguish between the different types of copyright work.
- It is no longer necessary for publicly accessible libraries to make a charge when copying for users, but where a charge is levied this must be in line with the costs of making the copy.
- The legislation no longer refers to 'prescribed libraries', because this has been replaced by the definition in section 43A which now covers librarians of a publicly accessible library or the library of an educational establishment – where these are not for profit.
- The exception for librarians to copy single copies of published works on behalf of their users specifies that this relates to the making of a single copy of a *reasonable proportion* of the work. There is nothing in the legislation which spells out more precisely what the phrase 'a reasonable proportion' actually means. It is for that reason that the details of the 2006 LACA/Ordnance Survey agreement are given above, because they do indicate what Ordnance Survey deemed to be acceptable to them under that agreement. But it should be remembered that the 2006 agreement pre-dates the changes which were made to the copyright exceptions during the course of 2014, and that one of those changes means that librarians are now able to copy artistic works (such as maps) on behalf of their users.

4.6.5.2 Copying maps – general points

It is possible for individual library users to copy maps under the copyright exceptions, but by their nature the copyright exceptions are narrow in scope. Indeed, at the time of the LACA/Ordnance Survey agreement, the OS explicitly accepted that the law does allow users to make fair dealing copies from artistic works, including mapping, for themselves, whether from paper or digital originals. Table 4.1 lists some of the main exceptions which might be used as the basis for copying maps. It shows whether the exception is subject to fair dealing, and whether it covers commercial use of the maps or only extends to non-commercial usage.

At the time the 2006 agreement was drawn up the law did not allow librarians and archivists to provide 'library privilege' copies of artistic works for users (except where an illustration was incidentally included with a text) unless licensed, which was what prompted the requirement at the time for the LACA/Ordnance Survey agreement.

Table 4.1 *Copying maps under the copyright exceptions*

	CDPA section number	Subject to Fair Dealing?	Limited to non-commercial?
Research	29(1)	Yes	Yes
Private study	29(1C)	Yes	Yes
Quotation	30(1ZA)	Yes	No
Illustration for instruction	32	Yes	Yes
Copying by librarians	42A	Reasonable proportion	Yes

Two further points about copyright in maps:

- Standalone maps and charts are excluded from CLA licences such as the HE licence or the business licence).
- Clause 3.1.5 of Digimap's terms and conditions covers the inclusion of maps in theses for library deposit where the use conforms to the customary and usual practice of the university (see the Edina site – Edina is a JISC designated service: http://digimap.edina.ac.uk/webhelp/os/copyright/licence_agreement. htm).

4.6.5.3   Lending of maps

The rental or lending of copyright-protected works is an act which is restricted to the rights holder. There are a couple of exceptions in the CDPA 1988 which deal with lending of works and they deal with lending by public libraries (s 40A) and by educational establishments (s 36A). As far as public libraries are concerned, it is not an infringement of a work to lend a book which is within the public lending right scheme. However, public libraries do not have an automatic right to lend maps. This is because they are only entitled to lend content under the CDPA exception in section 40A where it is covered by the public lending right scheme, and that scheme does *not* cover maps. In order to get the necessary authorization it would require some form of licence, but I am not aware of there being a map lending licence.

4.7   Licence disputes and their resolution

Before entering into a licence agreement it is worth spending some time thinking through what would happen in the event of a dispute, because that will help you to put in place a number of measures to make a dispute less likely; and should a dispute arise, the time that was taken to think things through during the licence negotiation process will mean that it is far clearer how things can be resolved.

At the time you negotiate the licence, if there is anything that you don't understand make sure that you get clarification. If the wording of the agreement is misleading, make sure that it is suitably changed before you sign up to the licence agreement. Ambiguous wording could potentially result in a dispute over the meaning of a particular word or phrase in the licence agreement. It is no use saying afterwards that you would never have signed up to the agreement if you had realized what it meant.

Does the agreement state the system of law which will be used to interpret the contract and to deal with any disputes arising from it? If that isn't the law of the country in which your institution is based, see if you can get it changed. If there isn't a clause specifying which courts have jurisdiction to settle any claim or dispute that might arise, this will need to be added to the agreement before it is signed.

Does the agreement provide an alternative dispute resolution mechanism which would be used if a dispute were to arise? It would set out a way of resolving potential disputes without necessarily having to take the matter to court. For example, if the matter cannot be resolved by negotiation, one option would be to include an alternative dispute resolution (ADR) clause where the matter would be referred to mediation in accordance with a model set of procedures such as the Centre for Effective Dispute Resolution's Model Mediation Procedure.[9] Another example would be where it was subject to binding arbitration under the Rules of Arbitration of the International Chamber of Commerce.[10] Agreeing a clause on an alternative dispute resolution mechanism as part of the licence agreement could save you a considerable amount of money.

If a dispute with the licensor does take place, the first thing to do would be to see if the matter can be resolved informally. Going to court or to a Tribunal would be a last resort.

No one wants to find themselves in a dispute over a copyright licence. But if you have spent time clarifying the meaning of the licence wording and negotiating the terms of the licence, both parties will have a clearer idea of their obligations under the agreement and that should make it less likely for a dispute to arise. So the time and effort spent negotiating the licence can be considered to be a good investment.

4.7.1 Disputes with collecting societies

If a licensee has a dispute with a collective licensing society, the matter can be referred to the Copyright Tribunal. The purpose of the Tribunal is to resolve disputes over the reasonableness of the terms of a licence from a collecting society. The Tribunal's rules of procedure are set out in The Copyright Tribunal Rules 2010: SI 2010/791. In order to commence proceedings, a person must file an application form, a statement of grounds and the relevant fee. The statement of grounds must contain a concise statement of the facts on which the applicant relies; the relevant statutory provision under which the application is made; where appropriate it will also include the payment terms or the licence terms which the applicant believes to be unreasonable; and it will also specify the relief sought. Anyone who has unreasonably been refused a licence by a collecting society or who considers the terms of a licence offered to them to be unreasonable may refer the matter to the Tribunal. Decisions of the Copyright Tribunal can be appealed to the High Court, but only on points of law.

Ombudsman Services (copyright licensing) can be used for disputes with collecting societies. But before a complaint can be accepted you must first have given the CMO a reasonable opportunity to resolve it. If you have received their final position regarding your complaint and you are still unhappy, or if eight weeks have passed and the complaint remains unresolved, Ombudsman Services may be able to help. In coming to a decision it would take account of both sides of the story; regulatory rules, guidance and standards; codes of practice, relevant law and regulations; and also what is accepted as good industry practice. Where a mistake has been made or where the customer has been treated unfairly, Ombudsman Services may require a participating company[11] to make a financial award to the complainant.[12] The most common time and trouble award is £50, and most awards are less than £100. Only in exceptional circumstances are time and trouble awards over £500. But Ombudsman Services is able to award up to £10,000 to return the complainant to the position that it would have been in had the circumstances which led up to the dispute not occurred. The Ombudsman Services terms of reference are available at www.ombudsman-services.org/downloads/OS_TermsofReference_from1October2013.pdf.

4.7.2   Disputes over the licensing of orphan works

Orphan works licence applicants can appeal to the IPO if they think that the IPO has made a mistake in refusing their application, a mistake in imposing a condition applied to the licence or a mistake in the licence fee quoted.

Where someone is unhappy with decisions of the Intellectual Property Office regarding the issuing of orphan works licences, they should first appeal to the IPO. If the aggrieved party is unhappy with the decision and response of the IPO to their appeal, they can refer the matter back to the IPO for a second time, whereupon an IPO manager will consider the matter; that person will not have been involved in the original decision, nor will they have been involved in the response to the first appeal. It is only once that process has been exhausted that licence applicants can appeal to the Copyright Tribunal. Rights holders can appeal to the First-tier Tribunal Regulatory Chamber.

Rights holders of orphan works can appeal to the IPO if they think that in reaching a decision the IPO has acted improperly or has failed to discharge its obligations under the regulations.

There is a route of appeal to the Copyright Tribunal for rights holders whose works have been used under the EU Directive (2012/28/EU). This is where disputes arise because the orphan works user and the rights holder cannot agree over the level of fair compensation.

4.8 UK Government Licensing Framework (The National Archives)

The UK Government Licensing Framework (GLF) provides a policy and legal overview of the arrangements for the licensing and re-use of public sector information. That would cover both central government information and that of the wider public sector. It sets out best practice and it also standardizes the licensing principles for government information. The GLF consists of three different types of licence: the Open Government Licence (Section 4.8.1 below), the Non-Commercial Government Licence (4.8.2), and the Charged Licence (4.8.3); and it recommends that the Open Government Licence should be the default licence for public sector information.

The National Archives maintains a list of public bodies which have Crown status, which means that the material they produce is subject to Crown copyright protection: www.nationalarchives.gov.uk/information-management/re-using-public-sector-information/copyright-and-re-use/uk-crown-bodies.

4.8.1 Open Government Licence

In September 2010, The National Archives launched the Open Government Licence. As a consequence, Crown copyright material, which was previously available for re-use under waiver conditions, can now be re-used under the terms of the Open Government Licence. At the time of writing the Open Government Licence is in its third iteration (www.nationalarchives.gov.uk/ doc/open-government-licence/version/3).

The Open Government Licence is part of the UK Government Licensing Framework:

- There are no charges or fees.
- There is no requirement to register or apply.
- It replaces the old click-use licence for Crown copyright material.

Under the terms of the Open Government Licence (www.nationalarchives.gov.uk/ doc/open-government-licence), users are free to:

- copy, publish, distribute and transmit the information
- adapt the information
- exploit the information commercially and non-commercially, for example, by combining it with other information, or by including it in their own product or application.

The information must have been expressly made available under the Open Government Licence. The licence is:

- worldwide
- royalty free
- perpetual
- non-exclusive.

There are a number of conditions that need to be met by users of Crown copyright material under the terms of the Open Government Licence:

- They must acknowledge the source of the information by including or linking to any attribution statement specified by the Information Provider(s) and, where possible, provide a link to the licence.
- They must not use the information in a way that suggests any official status or that the Information Provider and/or licensor endorses them or their use of the information.
- They must ensure that they do not mislead others or misrepresent the Information or its source.
- They must ensure that their use of the Information does not breach the Data Protection Act 1998 or the Privacy and Electronic Communications (EC Directive) Regulations 2003.

There are a number of exemptions. The licence does not cover:

- personal data in the information
- information that has not been accessed by way of publication or disclosure under information access legislation by or with the consent of the information provider
- departmental or public sector organization logos and crests and the royal arms, except where they form an integral part of a document or dataset
- military insignia
- third-party rights the information provider is not authorized to license
- other intellectual property rights, including patents, trade marks and design rights
- identity documents such as the British passport.

4.8.2   Non-Commercial Government Licence

Although the default position is that public sector information should be licensed for use and re-use free of charge under the Open Government Licence, there will be circumstances where it is appropriate for information to be released for use and re-use where this is only for non-commercial purposes. Where a public sector body licences its information under the Non-Commercial Government Licence, it will normally insert a visible statement asserting this and provide a link to the licence terms in the information.

4.8.3   Charged Licence[13]

The Charged Licence consists of standard licensing terms and, together with the above licences, forms part of the UK Government Licensing Framework.

Where a public authority charges a fee for the re-use of a dataset, it must do so in accordance with the Charged Licence.

4.9   Open Parliament Licence

Parliamentary copyright covers works which are made by or under the direction or control of the House of Commons or the House of Lords (see section 165 of the CDPA 1988). There is an Open Parliament Licence along similar lines to the Open Government Licence which encourages the use and re-use of information available under the licence. It does so freely and flexibly, but as with the Open Government Licence, there are a number of conditions that need to be observed.

The Open Parliament Licence does not override the exceptions for the making of copies such as those available for non-commercial research or private study. Indeed, along with a number of other exceptions, the section 29 exception contains a provision specifically ruling out the possibility of contract override. The Open Parliament Licence allows people to:

- copy, publish, distribute and transmit the information
- adapt the information
- exploit the information, whether commercially or non-commercially.

Material released under parliamentary copyright is, in most cases and unless otherwise stated, available to use without the permission of the copyright holder. This means you can copy, adapt, disseminate and reproduce the material without prior permission, as long as you acknowledge the source. Material which may be copied without prior permission or charge includes:

- Lords and Commons *Hansard*
- Command Papers
- reports of Select Committees of both Houses.

The Open Parliament Licence does *not* cover:

- personal data in the information
- information that has neither been published nor disclosed under information access legislation by or with the consent of the licensor
- material owned by third parties
- the Crowned Portcullis logo
- images featured on Art in Parliament
- parliamentary archives
- parliamentary photographic images
- live and archive video or audio broadcasts.

4.10   Creative Commons

Creative Commons is a non-profit organization that helps people to share their knowledge and creativity with the world. It does this through a number of free legal tools.

Creative Commons licences try to achieve a point in between two extremes – all rights reserved at one extreme, and no rights reserved at the other extreme. The licences try to make it as easy as possible to understand what they cover, by adopting four components, each with its own abbreviation and icon (see also Figure 4.2 on the next page):

- Attribution: **BY**
- No Derivative Works: **ND**
- Non-Commercial: **NC**
- Share Alike: **SA**

Each licence consists of a combination of these components:

CC BY	Attribution
CC BY-SA	Attribution, Share Alike
CC BY-ND	Attribution, No Derivative Works
CC BY-NC	Attribution, Non-Commercial
CC BY-NC-SA	Attribution, Non-Commercial, Share Alike
CC BY-NC-ND	Attribution, Non-Commercial, No Derivatives

Name	Explanation	Icon
Attribution	You let others copy, distribute, display, and perform your copyrighted work – and derivative works based upon it – but only if they give credit the way you request.	
Non-Commercial	You let others copy, distribute, display, and perform your work – and derivative works based upon it – but for non-commercial purposes only.	
No Derivative Works	You let others copy, distribute, display, and perform only verbatim copies of your work, not derivative works based upon it.	
Share Alike	You allow others to distribute derivative works only under a licence identical to the licence that governs your work.	

Figure 4.2 *Creative Commons icons and what they symbolize (the CC icons are taken from http://creativecommons.org/about/downloads under a CC BY licence, http://creativecommons.org/licenses/by/4.0)*

However, a licence cannot feature both the Share Alike and the No Derivative Works options. The Share Alike requirement applies only to derivative works.

Creative Commons licences are:

- **international** – the licences are intended to be legally effective everywhere.
- **irrevocable** – so once you receive material under a CC licence, you will always have the right to use it under those licence terms. As explained in 'On verifying the commons',[14] it doesn't mean that creators can't stop offering a work of theirs under the licence. Rather, it simply means that if a licensor changes the type of Creative Commons licence, anyone who comes across the work in the future will be bound by the new terms as opposed to the older ones. It does not mean, however, that for someone who found the work when it was made available under a different licence that this older licence is somehow invalidated.
- **enforceable** – the licence restrictions can and have been enforced through the courts, and there have been a number of legal cases in various jurisdictions around the world which demonstrate this:
  — In a 2010 Belgian Case Lichodmapwa were awarded €4500 for an infringement of their song *Abatchouck*, which had been released under a CC BY-NC-ND licence.
  — In 2008 Bulgarian blogger Elenko Elenkov filed a lawsuit against the newspaper *24 hours* for having one of his photos licensed under a CC BY-SA licence.
  — In 2006 Adam Curry sued *Weekend*, a Dutch tabloid – the publisher faces a fine of €1000 if it publishes any of Curry's pictures without permission again.

— In 2011 in the Israeli case of Avi Re'uveni v Mapa Inc. the defendant violated all three licence conditions (BY-NC-ND license) when she made a collage incorporating the photographs, sold the collages, and didn't provide attribution.

Creative Commons tries to make it as easy as possible for people to license content, and for the use of CC licensed works to be properly acknowledged, and there are a number of tools available to facilitate this. For example:

- Microsoft has a downloadable add-in (www.microsoft.com/en-gb/download/ ✷ details.aspx?id=13303) which enables users to embed Creative Commons licences directly into Word, Excel and PowerPoint documents.
- A tool is available called the Redact-O-Matic or Redactor (www.creativecommons.org.uk/redactor-automatically-find-cc-material-for-your-documents/), which offers users the ability to either redact sections of text from a document or to choose from a number of different options to redact images. It makes it easy to replace an image within the document you are working on with an alternative that has been licensed under Creative Commons.
- RDFA – Resource Description Framework in Attributes – is a tool which is being worked on with the World Wide Web Consortium (W3C). It isn't exclusive to the Creative Commons licences, but is instead a way of putting copyright and licensing information into HTML. It has the potential to revolutionize how content is moved around the web. RDFA can help anybody express who is the owner of the object and what is the licensing. If you were to copy and paste something which uses RDFA it means that the copyright and licensing information comes along with it.
- Open Attribute (http://openattribute.com) makes it easy to properly attribute ✷ CC licensed content.

4.11   GNU General Public Licence (open software)

The GNU General Public Licence (GPL) (www.gnu.org/licenses/gpl.html) is a widely used open source software licence. It is a free, 'copyleft' licence for software and other kinds of works which was originally written by Richard Stallman for the GNU project. The GPL licence grants the users irrevocable rights to use, modify and redistribute software, even commercially, on the proviso that software or its derivatives retain the GPL licence and that the source code is included or available to the user. An essential component of the GPL licence is the share alike feature, which must always be passed on. See clause 12 of the GPL version 3 (2007), entitled 'No Surrender of Others' Freedom':

If conditions are imposed on you (whether by court order, agreement or otherwise) that contradict the conditions of this License, they do not excuse you from the conditions of this License. If you cannot convey a covered work so as to satisfy simultaneously your obligations under this License and any other pertinent obligations, then as a consequence you may not convey it at all. For example, if you agree to terms that obligate you to collect a royalty for further conveying from those to whom you convey the Program, the only way you could satisfy both those terms and this License would be to refrain entirely from conveying the Program.

For further information, see Kuhn, B. M. et al. (2014) *Copyleft and the GNU General Public License: a comprehensive tutorial,* http://static.fsf.org/nosvn/cle/cle-2014-kuhn.pdf.

Notes

1 The Music Publishers Association owns two collecting societies – the Mechanical-Copyright Protection Society Ltd (MCPS) and Printed Music Licensing Ltd.

2 Bayley, E. (2009) *The Clicks That Bind: ways users 'agree' to online terms of service,* Electronic Frontier Foundation, https://www.eff.org/wp/clicks-bind-ways-users-agree-online-terms-service.

3 Newman, M. (2009) How Much? Textbook Writer Stung by Permission Fees, *Times Higher Education,* 7 August.

4 *An Economic Analysis of Copyright, Secondary Copyright and Collective Licensing,* PwC, March 2011.

5 The original ERA licence, which was under The Copyright (Certification of Licensing Scheme for Educational Recording of Broadcasts and Cable Programmes) (Educational Recording Agency Limited) Order 1990 (SI 1990/879), came into effect on 30 May 1990. See www.legislation.gov.uk/uksi/1990/879/made/data.pdf.

6 Ordnance Survey is Great Britain's national mapping agency. It is one of the four organizations which form the Public Data Group (https://www.gov.uk/government/groups/public-data-group).

7 www.ordnancesurvey.co.uk/business-and-government/products/opendata-products-grid.html.

8 www.cilip.org.uk/cilip/advocacy-awards-and-projects/advocacy-and-campaigns/copyright/copyright-briefings-and-3.

9 www.cedr.com/about_us/modeldocs/?id=21.

10 www.iccwbo.org/Products-and-Services/Arbitration-and-ADR/Arbitration/Rules-of-Arbitration/icc-Rules-of-Arbitration.

11 www.ombudsman-services.org/companies-copyright.html.

12 Ombudsman Services (2014) *Financial Awards: guidance for consumers,*

http://ombudsman-services.org/downloads/Financialawards_
guidanceforconsumers.pdf.

13   www.nationalarchives.gov.uk/documents/information-management/charged-
licence.pdf.

14   Benenson, F. (2008) *On Verifying the Commons*, 27 October,
http://creativecommons.org/weblog/entry/10296.

Digital copyright

Chapter 5 covers:

5.1   Copyright and the internet

A significant proportion of the information published on the internet can be said technically to be freely available. In some cases, though, information is not freely available on the internet:

- because it is only available behind a paywall, or
- because the information is only available to registered users of a website.

The internet is definitely not a copyright-free zone. Even where information is *technically* freely available to navigate and browse around and to print, download, or copy and paste, this does not mean that it is automatically possible *from a legal standpoint* to copy without restriction in whatever way and to whatever extent an internet user wishes. It is safest to work on the assumption that works on the internet are protected by copyright, unless there is something to indicate otherwise, such as a public domain symbol.

Copyright protects content automatically, without the need for the copyright owner to go through a registration process. As long as it is original, fixed, and falls into one of the categories or 'species' protected by UK copyright law (literary, dramatic, musical or artistic works; sound recordings, films and broadcasts) then the work will be protected from the moment that it has been created. There is no requirement to place a copyright symbol on the work or to put some sort of copyright notice or statement on it in order to get protection.

In the case of a website, this would not be protected as an entity in its own right, but the constituent parts that make up the website will instead be protected individually. So, for example, if there were a web page consisting of text wrapped around an image; and if the page plays a piece of music once it has loaded:

- the text will be protected as a literary work
- the image will be protected as an artistic work
- the piece of music will be protected as a musical work
- the metadata will be protected as a literary work
- there is also the exclusive right of the rights holder to communicate their work to the public (by electronic means).

If you wish to use content on a website, the first thing to do would be to look if there is anything to indicate the copyright situation, and what it says is permitted:

- Is there a link with a heading such as 'Copyright', 'Terms and conditions' or 'Legal and disclaimer'?
- Is there something to indicate that it is issued under a Creative Commons licence?
- Is there a public domain symbol?

There could be a copyright statement on the site as a whole, on the individual page you wish to copy from, or within a document appearing on that page (such as an MS Word or Adobe PDF document). The statement won't necessarily use 'copyright' as the heading; it could instead be called something like 'terms and conditions', 'legal statement', 'terms of service' or 'legal and disclaimer'. If there is no copyright symbol or copyright statement on the web page that you want to copy from, you cannot automatically assume that the copyright owner is happy for people to use the content in any way they wish.

5.1.1   Implied licences

In some cases one might argue that there is an implied licence to copy material from a website. It would, however, be dangerous to automatically assume that this will be the case by default. Ask yourself the question: 'What makes you think that there is an implied licence to copy?'

If a website has an icon or button saying 'Print', 'Download' or 'E-mail to a friend', you could say that the site is giving you an implied licence to do precisely that. However, that doesn't mean that you have the right to do whatever you want with the content. It wouldn't, for example, give you the right to post that content in its entirety on your own website, or make it available for sale.

There is, however, another problem to consider. How can you be sure that the material that you are looking at has been placed there lawfully? Or to put it another way, what if the copy has been placed there without the knowledge or permission of the copyright holder and is therefore an infringing copy?

There is a real disconnection between on the one hand the ease with which digital content on the internet can technically be used, copied, re-used, embedded, mashed up, mined or textually analysed; and on the other hand the complexities of copyright protection which make it difficult to resolve the rights clearance issues. Internet users see and experience the ease with which information and data can technically be used and re-used and inevitably their expectations are that the legal ability to copy material should and will be equally straightforward.

There are a number of reasons why copyright is complex when applied to content on the internet:

- Copyright consists of a bundle of rights:
  — reproduction right
  — making available right
  — communication to the public right
  — performers' rights.
- Copyright is a territorial right.
- There is also the question of jurisdiction – where did the infringement occur, and where should copyright be enforced?

Google,[1] in its response to the EU's 2013 'Public consultation on the review of the EU copyright rules', has said that 'In a sensible licensing market, distinguishing between rights does not make sense where there is a single act of exploitation'. They argue that there should be a single fee to pay for what they consider to be a single act of exploitation, rather than multiple fees payable to cover what are treated as multiple rights. They say that because the scope of the making available right is unclear, it frequently overlaps with other economic rights and as a consequence a video platform can be charged for multiple rights: reproduction, communication to the public, and making available, while due to disputes about where the video is 'made available' and who owns what rights in which territories, the video may be blocked in a number of member states. All of this can lead to multiple payments being made or an inability to license. For further information, see Sari Depreeuw and Jean-Benoit Hubin (2014) *Study on the Making Available*

Right and its Relationship with the Reproduction Right in Cross-Border Digital Transmissions, De Wolf & Partners, European Union, ISBN 978-92-79-33045-2.

5.2   Communication to the public

'Communication to the public' by electronic transmission is a restricted act. Section 20 of the CDPA 1988 deals with infringement by communication to the public. A combination of the wording in the legislation, and the decisions from European Court of Justice cases, helps us to understand what is meant by the phrase 'communication to the public'. It includes:

- broadcasting the work
- making the work available by electronic means in a way that members of the public could access it from a place and at a time individually chosen by them.

The meaning of 'communication to the public' has also been further clarified by case law:

- Streaming is a communication to the public (ITV v TV Catchup).
- Hyperlinking is a communication to the public (Svensson C-466/12), but this would only infringe if it were a communication to a <u>new</u> public (see Section 5.3.1 below).

CJEU case law also tells us that:

- A communication by hotels to hotel bedrooms is a communication to the public (SGAE/Rafael Hoteles C-306/05 and Public Performance (Ireland) v Ireland, Attorney General (C-162/10)).
- A dentist who broadcasts phonograms free of charge in his private dental practice isn't making a 'communication to the public', and such broadcasting doesn't therefore give rise to the remuneration right (See SCF v Marco Del Corso C-135/10). The sole reason why patients attended the dental practice was in order to receive dental treatment. There would only ever be a very small number of people at the practice at any one time. As there would be a steady flow of people, they would each hear different phonograms being broadcast. The broadcasts would be enjoyed by clients without them having made any active choice. And finally, the broadcasts were not of a profit-making nature.
- A spa which transmits protected musical works to its guests by means of television and radio sets located in the bedrooms of its guests carries out a communication to the public of those works. As such it must pay copyright fees because a communication to the public of that kind has to be authorized

by the authors who must in principle receive adequate compensation (Ochranný svaz autorský pro práva k dílům hudebním o.s. (OSA) v Léčebné lázně Mariánské Lázně a.s. (C-351/12)).

5.3 Hyperlinking and embedding
5.3.1 Hyperlinks

It may seem as though this is self-evident, but a communication to the public requires both a *communication* and a *public*. Hyperlinks do make the works that they are linking to available, and are therefore an act of communication. However, the public that the content is being communicated or made available to requires consideration, too. It would only be a problem if the hyperlink communicated the material to a new public.

The CJEU case of Nils Svensson and others v Retriever Sverige AB (C-466/12) found that a hyperlink is a communication to the public. However, such a communication to the public was permitted as long as this was not a communication to a new public which wasn't envisaged by the rights holder. An example of where the communication would have been to a new public is where the link circumvents restrictions put in place by the site on which the protected work appears (such as a paywall or a log-in screen), and where this has been done without permission. Another example would be linking to the content where the work is no longer available to the public on the site on which it was initially communicated or where it is henceforth available on that site only to a restricted public. That could, for example, happen where you link to the content on a cached version of the web page, having done so because you know that it is no longer available on the live version of that page.

There may be a need for future case law to help us interpret and clarify what would be considered to be freely available.

The following are key points to consider when creating hyperlinks:

- You can create hyperlinks to third-party content without the authorization of the copyright holder.
- The work must still be publicly available on the original site.
- You must not link to unauthorized content.
- You must not circumvent technical measures which control access to content.

5.3.2 Embedding

The Svensson case (C-466/12) found that framed text links were permitted. Inline frames or Iframes can be used to display content from a third-party website on your own site. The BestWater International GmbH v Michael Mebes and Stefan

Potsch (C-348/13) case confirms that embedding of copyright-protected content on a third-party website is alright because it would not reach 'a new public', unless the original publisher has made use of technical access restrictions.

Together these European Court of Justice judgments mean that it is possible to use inline frames in order to embed into your own website videos, audio files or image files that are hosted on a third-party website. The onus would therefore seem to be on the rights holder to implement restrictive technical measures or paywalls to limit access from the outset, because any communication to the public by someone other than the rights holder would then be communicating that content to a new public – i.e. to a public beyond that originally envisaged by the rights holder.

Before the Bestwater judgment, the German collecting society GEMA had been calling for internet users to be required to pay a licensing fee in order to be able to embed copyright-protected videos, such as YouTube videos, on websites. If the European Court of Justice had found in the Bestwater case that a licence fee was required to be able to frame or embed other people's content, there would then have been a number of practical issues to consider, because it would have led to the possibility of a site like YouTube needing a licence for users to be able to watch videos, and also for the end-user to pay a fee if they were to embed those videos into their sites.

If you are the owner of copyright in a work, and you do not want people to create deep links to your content, or if you do not wish them to embed your work in their site:

- use a robust set of terms and conditions
- use technical measures to prevent people from being able to embed your work within their site.

5.4   Database right

Directive 96/9/EC on the legal protection of databases, which was implemented in the UK through The Copyright and Rights in Databases Regulations 1997: SI 1997/3032 introduced a new right known as 'database right'.

Databases are protected as a 'species' for the purposes of database right but they aren't necessarily digital. The right protects both print and electronic databases, because Regulation 6 of the statutory instrument inserts section 3A into the CDPA 1988, which contains a definition of 'database' as follows:

In this Part "database" means a collection of independent works, data or other materials which –

(a)   are arranged in a systematic or methodical way, and

(b)   are individually accessible by electronic or other means

Source: The National Archives, 2015

The crucial wording is that the database is individually accessible by electronic *or other means*. It could include websites, printed directories, encyclopaedias or online statistical databases.

To qualify for database right substantial investment must have taken place in

- obtaining,
- verifying and
- presenting

the contents of the database. Investment includes any investment, whether of financial, human or technical resources, but it must be clearly distinguishable from the investment that has been made in the creation of the data. Database right only protects the investment in the collation, arrangement and presentation of the contents of the database.

Where a database qualifies for database right, the right prevents the unauthorized extraction and/or re-utilization of the whole or a substantial part of the database (and, in certain circumstances, the repeated and systematic extraction/re-utilization of insubstantial parts, where they would together be considered to be a substantial part).

- 'Extraction' means the transfer of the contents of the database to another medium.
- 'Re-utilization' means making available to the public the contents of a database.

In order for a database to qualify for copyright protection it must be original, and it can only be considered to be original if 'by reason of the selection or arrangement of the contents of the database the database constitutes the author's own intellectual creation' (CDPA 1988 s3A (2)). Putting together an A–Z listing doesn't involve the author's own intellectual creation.

Unauthorized extraction and/or re-utilization of the whole or a substantial part of a protected database will amount to an infringement. A substantial part of a database can be assessed quantitatively and/or qualitatively. A quantitative assessment looks at the volume of data extracted in relation to the total volume of the database. A qualitative assessment looks at the scale of investment in the obtaining, verification or presentation of the contents of the part of the database that has been extracted and/or re-utilized. Repeated and systematic extraction and/or re-utilization of insubstantial parts of a protected database can still amount to an infringement of the database right: (a) if the cumulative effect would lead to a 'reconstitution' of the database as a whole or, at the very least, a substantial part of it; and (b) if such acts conflict with the normal exploitation of a database or unreasonably prejudice the legitimate economic interest of the creator of the database.

5.4.1   Duration of protection

Copyright in a database lasts for 70 years from the end of the year of death of the author, if there is one, or the end of the year of first publication if there is no personal author. Database right gives protection for 15 years against extraction and re-utilization of the whole or a substantial part of the contents of the database. But any substantial changes to the database during this time (additions, deletions or alterations) which result in a further substantial investment, will give rise to a further 15-year extension.

5.4.2   Exceptions or permitted acts

Lawful users of a database are authorized to do anything necessary for them to be able to access and use the contents – even if there is a term or condition in any contract accompanying the database which purports to prohibit or restrict this lawful use, that clause in the agreement can be ignored.

The main exception to database right is that of fair dealing, and the database regulations make clear that fair dealing in the database right is permitted provided that:

- the person extracting the material is a lawful user of the database
- the purpose is illustration for teaching or research and not for any commercial purpose
- the source is indicated or acknowledged.

Tucked away towards the end of the database regulations, there are more exceptions to database right which are listed in schedule 1, and they cover public administration:

- parliamentary and judicial proceedings
- Royal Commissions and statutory inquiries
- material open to public inspection or on official register
- material communicated to the Crown in the course of public business
- public records
- acts done under statutory authority.

British Horseracing Board v William Hill (C-203/02)

This was the first real test of database right, although the topic had been touched upon in earlier court cases.

The British Horseracing Board (BHB) maintained a database which was constantly updated. Indeed, the cost of continuing to obtain, verify and present the contents of the database was approximately £4 million per year, involving about 80 staff and extensive computer software and hardware. The database contained details of over a million horses. It consisted of some 214 tables, altogether containing over 20 million records. An estimated total of 800,000 new records or changes to existing records were made each year.

Initially, the British Horseracing Board won a High Court challenge against William Hill over the use of pre-race data. BHB had argued that internet bookmakers who wished to use information such as runners and riders should pay a copyright fee. However, the case then went to the Court of Appeal, and in May 2002 the Court of Appeal referred a number of questions to the European Court of Justice.

When the European Court of Justice finally delivered its judgment in November 2004, it ruled that William Hill's use of horseracing data did not after all infringe the BHB's database rights. This came as something of a surprise to people following the case, because the earlier Advocate General's opinion had been quite favourable to database owners.

The CJEU said that the BHB did not have database right in its database of horseracing data because it had not made a sufficient investment in obtaining the contents of the database. According to the CJEU, 'obtaining' means 'seeking out existing independent materials' rather than 'the creation of materials'.

The BHB had spent considerable time and effort creating the data but the CJEU found that this was simply part of the process of putting together the pre-race information, including name, place and length of races, and details of the horses, and that it did not represent 'investment in . . . obtaining'.

Directmedia Publishing GmbH v Albert Ludwigs Universität Freiburg (C-304/07)

This case deals with the extent to which Directmedia used and relied upon an anthology of poems by the University of Freiburg. The Freiburg anthology, a collection of verse from 1720 to 1933, was published as part of a project under the overall direction of Professor Knoop at Albrecht Ludwigs Universität Freiburg. For the anthology a list of verse titles was drawn up – 'The 1100 most important poems in German literature between 1730 and 1900'. It took two and a half years to complete at a cost of €34,900. Directmedia published a CD-ROM in 2002 called '1000 poems everyone should have'. Professor Knoop and the University of Freiburg took the view that Directmedia had infringed the copyright of Professor Knoop and the related right of the University of Freiburg as maker of a database.

Directmedia didn't replicate exactly the same list of poems. Rather, they made their own assessment as to what should be included, and they submitted that there was no extraction if the database was merely used as a source of information.

The CJEU judgment published in October 2008 tells us that the database right can be infringed if the copy is made by technical means but that it can also be infringed where the copying is done through manual copying of the contents:

> . . . it is immaterial, for the purposes of assessing whether there has been an 'extraction', within the meaning of Article 7 of Directive 96/9, that the transfer is based on a technical process of copying the contents of a protected database, such as

electronic, electromagnetic or electro-optical processes or any other similar processes . . .
or on a simple manual process . . . even a manual recopying of the contents of such a
database to another medium corresponds to the concept of extraction in the same way as
downloading or photocopying

Paragraph 37 of the judgment

The judgment also makes it absolutely clear that an infringement of database right doesn't have
to involve the making of a direct copy without adaptation.

It is also immaterial, for the purposes of interpreting the concept of extraction in the
context of Directive 96/9, that the transfer of the contents of a protected database may
lead to an arrangement of the elements concerned which is different from that in the
original database.

Paragraph 39 of the judgment

5.5   Archiving and preservation of digital content

There are a number of changes which came into effect in June 2014 which make
it easier for libraries to preserve content in digital form. The first of these is the
new exception in section 40B which allows educational establishments, libraries,
archives and museums to offer access to all types of copyright works by dedicated
terminals on the premises for the purposes of research or private study. The
second is the revised wording of the exception in section 42, which now allows
publicly accessible libraries, archives or museums to make copies of any types of
work for the purposes of preservation or replacement.

The section 40B exception[2] is limited to works which have been lawfully
acquired; where they are communicated or made available to individual members
of the public for the purposes of research or private study, and where there are any
purchasing or licensing terms, these must be complied with. In other words, this
exception does not override the wording of contractual terms.

The dedicated terminals exception is especially useful as a way of providing
access to works which are either too fragile to handle, or where they have already
been preserved in digital form. There is the added benefit for those with a visual
impairment that once a work has been converted into digital form it is easy to
zoom in and enlarge pages as required.

The section 42 exception[3] would cover where a work has become worn or
damaged and therefore needs to be copied in order to ensure its long-term
preservation. It would also cover making copies for other publicly accessible
libraries where they had a copy in their permanent collection but where that copy
has either been lost, destroyed or damaged.

The preservation exception is limited to where it is an item in a collection that is kept entirely or mainly for on-site reference purposes or where it is not accessible to the public or where it is only available for loan to other libraries, archives or museums (as opposed to being available for loan to individual library users).

5.6 Mass digitization

In 2011 the European Commission adopted a recommendation (2011/711/EU) on the digitization and online accessibility of cultural material and digital preservation. In its report'[4] the European Commission concluded that digitization of works in Europe remains a challenge.

5.6.1 The Re-Use of Public Sector Information Directive

Recital 30 of Directive 2013/37/EU, which amends Directive 2003/98/EC on the re-use of public sector information, acknowledges the role public–private partnerships can play in helping to make our cultural heritage available in digital form:

> There are numerous cooperation arrangements between libraries, including university libraries, museums, archives and private partners which involve digitization of cultural resources granting exclusive rights to private partners. Practice has shown that such public–private partnerships can facilitate worthwhile use of cultural collections and at the same time accelerate access to the cultural heritage for members of the public.

As a result, the legislation recognizes the importance of the role that public–private partnerships can play in facilitating the digitization of content. Digitization projects can involve high costs, and recital 31 of Directive 2013/37/EU acknowledges that libraries and archives may need to enter into an exclusive agreement with a private partner as a way for the private partner to be able to recoup the monies that they invest in digitizing the content. However, where exclusive agreements are used, the period of exclusivity should be as short as possible, and it is limited under the directive to a maximum of ten years.

The Re-Use of Public Sector Information Regulations 2015 (SI 2015/1415) implement Directive 2013/37/EU which in turn amends Directive 2003/98/EC on the reuse of public sector information.

5.6.2 Digitization of orphan works

Where a mass digitization project is undertaken, there will almost inevitably be a number of works for which it is impossible to identify or locate the rights holders, even after a thorough and diligent search has been carried out, and these are known as 'orphan works'.

Since October 2014 there have been a number of solutions in place to enable orphan works to be digitized lawfully – those solutions consist of an exception covering certain permitted uses of orphan works (s 44B of the CDPA 1988), and also the use of licences (which can either be issued by the Intellectual Property Office or which could potentially be issued by collecting societies where they have been approved to offer extended collective licensing schemes).

All of the orphan works solutions require a diligent search to be undertaken. And it is questionable whether these are really scaleable solutions for projects involving the mass digitization of collections. There are several reasons why the orphan works solutions may actually stand in the way of, rather than encourage, digitization:

- The maximum period for which an orphan works licence will be issued is seven years.
- Once the licence has come to an end it would need to be renewed, and it would require another diligent search to be undertaken.
- The diligent search process is time-consuming, bureaucratic, and where it involves licences for the commercial use of the orphan works, the costs can be prohibitive.

5.6.3   Digitization by libraries

Publicly accessible not-for-profit libraries, as well as educational establishments, museums and archives, are able to digitize material and make it available to on-site users via dedicated terminals under section 40B of the CDPA 1988 (see also Section 3.3.3 on p. 53 for further information).

The European Court of Justice case Technische Universität Darmstadt v Eugen Ulmer KG (C-117/13) does provide us with some pointers to the extent to which libraries can rely on the exception. The CJEU confirmed the ancillary right of public libraries to digitize books from their collection in order to make them available by dedicated terminals without the rights holder's consent. However, in the opinion of the Court, this right does not allow publicly accessible libraries to digitize their entire collections. In any case, the right to make available content on dedicated terminals is subject to the purchasing and licensing terms that the material was issued under (i.e. where an agreement has been concluded with the rights holder).

The Court gives the (ancillary) right of digitization a very narrow scope by limiting it on the 'condition of specificity'. According to the court, this right is only applicable to 'some of the works of a collection' when it is necessary for the purposes outlined in Article 5(3)(n) of Directive 2001/29/EC. The 'necessity' of the digitization should be evaluated based on the three-step test envisaged in Article 5(5) of the Directive. The court explicitly underscores that the ancillary right of digitization does not allow publicly accessible libraries to digitize their entire collections (points 45, 46).

It remains unclear whether, provided the conditions of the three-step test are met, digitization of a substantial volume of the works in the library's collection is lawful.

Libraries may also rely on licences with collecting societies for the necessary authorization to digitize content. However, the licence terms would need to be thoroughly checked to establish precisely what they do and don't allow. If one were to take the example of the CLA's standard business licence, it would permit a company which has a current licence to store the digitized item on a shared area such as the firm's intranet, but this would be limited to a maximum of 30 days.

Libraries need to think through the benefits and disbenefits of the options available to them. These include the following points:

- The orphan works exception in section 44B of the CDPA 1988 (which implements Directive 2012/28/EU) does not cover the digitization of standalone images.
- The orphan works licences are only issued for a maximum of seven years at a time.

5.7   Licensing of electronic resources

Most electronic resources such as online databases, e-books and e-journals are made available through licence agreements. Access is therefore allowed in accordance with the licence terms.

There are some copying activities which are permitted under the exceptions in the CDPA 1988 which cannot be overridden by contracts or licences. You may make a copy for:

- research and private study
- text and data analysis
- quotation
- caricature, parody or pastiche
- a disabled person
- illustration for instruction
- supplying single copies to other libraries.

These exceptions are limited in scope (and the limits of each of them are outlined in Chapter 3). You may not:

- remove, modify or hide any copyright notices
- share material with unauthorized users
- systematically download.

It is important to ensure that you comply with the terms of the licence agreement for the electronic resource, otherwise the vendor could cut off access, citing a breach of contract. At the time of signing up to the licence agreement check that you will have direct access to the usage data for the product, because if that is not the case it is advisable to incorporate a clause in the contract requiring the account manager to provide you with the usage information on a regular basis. By having direct access to the usage data you will be able to spot at an early stage if there are any unusual patterns of usage, and to take the appropriate action (such as disabling a user ID, or changing the password for a user ID). Sometimes there can be genuine misunderstandings. For example, if your organization has a proxy server and the vendor isn't aware of this, the vendor may think that one user is making a huge number of downloads, and may disable your institution's account as a result.

5.8   Digital rights management systems

A digital rights management (DRM) system consists of both a technical protection measure (TPM) and rights management information (RMI). This can be expressed as TPM + RMI = DRM. The term digital rights management has also been referred to as digital restrictions management.

Libraries have warned that DRM systems make it impossible to gain access to works even for legitimate reasons. They can hinder the ability of libraries to preserve digital works in perpetuity, because it is likely that in future there would be no key available to unlock the digital rights management system.

Table 5.1 on the next page shows a few examples of how digital rights management systems have affected the provision of library services.

5.8.1   Technological protection measures complaints process

Technological protection measures (TPMs) (also known as copy protection measures) are often used to protect copyright works, for example, through the use of encryption on DVDs. TPMs can have an important role in enabling copyright owners (rights holders) to offer content to consumers in different ways, as well as protecting against unlawful copying (piracy). EU and UK law secures the right of copyright owners to use TPMs to protect their works, and consequently the circumvention of such technology is illegal.

The use of TPMs could, however, potentially prevent activities that are permitted by the copyright exceptions. The law therefore provides for a complaints process that aims to ensure that a TPM does not unreasonably prevent people from benefiting from an exception.

Article 6(4) of the Copyright Directive (2001/29/EC) does say that

> Member States shall take appropriate measures to ensure that rightsholders make available to the beneficiary of an exception or limitation provided for in national law . . . the means of benefiting from that exception or limitation . . . Where that beneficiary has legal access to the protected work . . .

Table 5.1 *Examples of how DRM systems have affected libraries*

In brief	In detail
E-book suppliers employ digital rights management to ensure that the e-book file destroys itself after three weeks.	In *The Modernisation Review of Public Libraries: a policy statement* (DCMS, 2010), it says that current e-book arrangements in libraries involve downloading from services such as Overdrive for e-book supply from libraries and that the scheme employs digital rights management so that the file destroys itself after three weeks.
Amazon's Kindle operates a closed digital rights management system which means that public libraries encounter problems with interoperability.	Amazon's Kindle devices operate a closed digital rights management system and as a result, public libraries are unable to purchase e-books in the Kindle format (as stated on library service websites such as those for Stockton Council, Slough Borough Council, Essex County Council and Middlesbrough Council). The Middlesbrough Council Libraries and Information website says that this is because Amazon doesn't allow e-books in the e-PUB format to be compatible with the Kindle (www.middlesbrough.gov.uk/CHttpHandler.ashx?id=12106&p=0).
The British Library uses digital rights management in order to deliver journal articles requested from their inter-library loans service.	In 2010 Peter Murray-Rust made an FOI request to the British Library (BL) in which he queried why the BL uses technical protection measures in its delivery of journal articles for inter-library loan, especially given their stance against the use of digital rights management systems by publishers (see www.whatdotheyknow.com/request/digital_rights_management_on_ele).

The response cited publishers' concerns over users cancelling subscriptions and using document suppliers instead; potential loss of revenue if articles became freely available on the web; and the fact that the use of TPM ensures that only a single copy is supplied in compliance with the CDPA (at the time it was ss 38 and 39 of the Act, although these sections have now been replaced by s 42A). |

Where a librarian is unable to benefit from one of the available exceptions because of being prevented from doing so by the publisher's use of a TPM, they should in the first instance contact the publisher to see if the matter can be resolved amicably. If a solution cannot be found which is agreeable to both the publisher and the librarian as the user of their content, there is a formal complaints process operated by the Intellectual Property Office.

The IPO's guidance does expect the user to try to negotiate a solution with the copyright owner before seeking assistance from the government. Indeed, it is a requirement of the complaints process that complainants answer whether they have attempted to do this, and if so, to show how they have done so. The guidelines published by the Intellectual Property Office on how the Secretary of State will deal ★ with the complaints which he/she might receive under the provisions of section 296ZEA of the CDPA 1988 can be found at www.gov.uk/government/publications/technological-protection-measures-tpms-complaints-process.

The Secretary of State would not want to impose a large and disproportionate burden on business and undermine the ability of the creative industries to produce content. Equally, the Secretary of State will also want to ensure that the benefits of the exceptions can be realized.

★   There is now a complaint form for potential complainants to fill in and it covers not only the Secretary of State's new power under section 296ZEA (on the making of personal copies for private use) but also the matching power that already existed under section 296ZE (in respect of a range of other exceptions): www.gov.uk/government/uploads/system/uploads/attachment_data/file/369992/tp m-complaints-form.pdf.

To be eligible for the complaints process the following conditions must apply to your complaint:

* The work you are complaining about must be a work that is protected by copyright (but not a computer program).
* You must have lawful access to the work. For example, you may own a lawful copy of the work, having bought it or been given it as a gift.
* To rely on the personal copying exception, you must have lawfully acquired the work on a permanent basis. This does not cover works that are borrowed, rented, accessed from on-demand streaming services or broadcasts.
* The TPM must be preventing you from benefiting from one of the *eligible* exceptions.

What does having lawful access to the work mean? Could the requirement of having lawful access be met by relying on a library copy? In the case of section 28B an individual is able to make a copy, but the law requires that they have lawfully *acquired* a copy of the work, and have done so on a *permanent basis*. Having access in a local public library certainly would not meet these requirements.

In the case of all the other eligible copyright exceptions (CDPA sections 29, 29A, 31A, 31B, 31BA, 32, 35, 36, 41, 42, 42A, 43, 44, 45, 46, 47, 48, 49, 50, 61, 68, 69, 70, 71 or section 75), you must have lawful access to the work. This could be through having bought it or having been given it as a gift. And it could potentially be argued that having access in a library meets the requirement. However, I am not aware of this having been tested either through the IPO's complaints process or through the courts. Arguing that library access to the work fully satisfies the requirement of having lawful access could be problematic. What if a library user were to make a complaint to the Secretary of State about a work which they knew was accessible in their local library; what if the Secretary of State's decision took quite a while to be announced, and what if in the meantime the library for whatever reason no longer had access to the work which was the subject of the complaint?

Complainants would be required to explain how they are entitled in law to benefit from the exception that they are relying upon, as well as outlining the permitted act that they have been prevented from carrying out by the protection measure applied to the work. Before making use of the complaints process the complainant must have already contacted the rights holder and tried to reach an amicable solution and as part of making use of the TPM complaints process they would be required to set out the steps that they have already taken to try and agree a solution with the rights holder.

From a practical perspective one has to ask:

- Would the moment of need for the information have long since passed by the time a decision has been reached?
- How would a favourable decision be enforced?
- Is it really worth the time and effort required to assert your rights?

What is clear is that you cannot use the TPM complaints process to complain about the inability to undertake a permitted act relating to software. It is a point worth emphasizing, because there have been a number of complaints to the Secretary of State which have been ineligible on the grounds that they relate to software.

5.9   Digital goods and the concept of exhaustion

The CJEU established in Oracle v Usedsoft (Case C-128/1) that the distribution right in article 4(2) of the Software Directive can in certain circumstances be exhausted. That would apply to software on a CD as well as software in the form of digital files downloaded from the internet with the rights holder's consent. It means that software can potentially be sold second-hand. But the Usedsoft case tells us that at the time of the sale, the original purchaser must delete any copy which he has made for his own use.

The Oracle v Usedsoft judgment inevitably raises the question of whether the principle of exhaustion can also apply to other digital works protected by copyright, such as audiobooks, films, music or video files.

In 2014 in a German case the Court of Appeal of Hamm backed the findings of the District Court of Bielefeld, which had ruled that the InfoSoc Directive (2001/29/EC) clearly and consciously excludes exhaustion for all the other types of digital content. There is no exhaustion of copyright in digital goods other than software, according to the Hamm Court of Appeal. And this is the case even where the content has been transferred onto a CD or other physical medium.

5.10   Rental and lending of digital content

Library 'e-lending' usually refers to the downloading of digital text from a website. This could technically be done remotely or on-site from within the library premises.

EBLIDA's 'Right to E-read' campaign site (www.eblida.org/e-read/home-campaign) says that

> Libraries guarantee free access to content, information, and culture for all European citizens. However, in the digital environment, the current legal framework prevents libraries from fulfilling these essential services to our society, especially regarding the provision of e-books.

There are several issues relating to e-books that have caused consternation for public libraries:

* Not all e-books are available for libraries to purchase.
* Publishers place restrictions on how libraries can offer them to their users.
* The price charged to libraries may be much higher than the cost for consumers.

The legal position regarding e-lending by libraries is currently in a state of flux. Case law in this area will help to clarify the situation. For example, in September 2014 the Court of Appeal of the Hague decided to refer preliminary questions on the lending of e-books to the European Court of Justice (VOB, Vereniging Openbare Bibliotheken) (Dutch Association of Public Libraries) v Stichting Leenrecht (CaseC-174/15)), but at the time of writing the CJEU's judgment was still awaited.

5.10.1   The legal restrictions

In the UK the remote downloading of e-books from the library has been questioned because of EU copyright law (2001/29/EC). The Digital Economy Act 2010 defines 'lent out' in section 43 of the Act:

(a)   Means made available to a member of the public for use away from library premises for a limited time, but

(b)   Does not include being communicated by means of electronic transmission to a place other than library premises . . .

Source: The National Archives, 2015

In its *Report under the Public Libraries and Museums Act 1964 for 2014*, published in December 2014, the UK Department of Culture, Media and Sport says that due to current EU copyright law it isn't possible to extend PLR payments to the remote lending of e-books but they point to the public consultation on a review of the EU's copyright rules which could allow it to be extended in the future to cover the remote lending of e-books. Changes to EU copyright law are envisaged, but as these are the subject of much debate it is impossible to say precisely which changes will make it into law. William Sieghart's *Independent Library Report for England*, published in December 2014, says that an action for central government is 'to seek to secure changes in European and UK copyright law to enable the public lending right to include remote e-loans in its next legislative term'.

5.10.2   Availability of e-books to libraries

Publishers aren't under any obligation in EU law to issue libraries with licences for them to lend out e-books. Some content is only available in digital form. So, the fact that a large number of e-books cannot currently be accessed through public libraries means that a significant amount of this type of information, knowledge and ideas is cut off from families, communities and businesses. According to http://shelffree.org.uk/page/3, of the 50 best-selling e-books of 2012, 85% were not made available by publishers for libraries to provide.

5.10.3   Publisher restrictions on the use of e-books

One business model – from HarperCollins – worked on the basis that it only allowed e-books to be borrowed 26 times, after which the library would have to buy another licence. The publisher's logic was that it was mimicking the print world, where a book would be so worn and falling to bits that it would need to be replaced after that number of loans[5].

The terms under which the e-book is lent may be dictated by a purchase agreement, a licence, or indeed by the library itself. This could cover the number of simultaneous users permitted, or the period for which the book can be issued out on loan.

5.10.4   The prices libraries are charged for e-books

As e-books are not owned by the library, but are instead licensed to them by the vendor or publisher, the publisher can impose differential pricing for different customers. The cost to libraries can be significantly more than the cost for consumers to buy the e-book. It could, for example, cost five times as much for a library to buy an e-book, because the library pricing will have been devised in order to take account of the anticipated way in which it would be lent out to lots of different library users. This is a similar principle to the way in which films might be made available to libraries as 'rental copies' at a higher price in order for them to be able to lend copies of films/DVDs.

5.10.5   Further information on e-lending

- IFLA (2014) IFLA, 2014 e-lending Background Paper.
- EBLIDA (2014) *The Right to E-read*, www.eblida.org/e-read/home-campaign.
- CILIP (2013) *Let Libraries Lend E-Books*, www.cilip.org.uk/cilip/advocacy-campaigns/e-books/let-libraries-lend-e-books.

Notes

1   Google, 2014, in its response to the public consultation on the review of the EU copyright rules, http://ec.europa.eu/internal_market/consultations/2013/copyright-rules/index_en.htm.
2   For further information on the section 40B exception on libraries and educational establishments making works available through dedicated terminals, see Section 3.3.3, p. 53.
3   For further information on the section 42 exception on copying by librarians: replacement copies of works, see section 3.3.5, p. 55.
4   European Commission (2014) *Cultural Heritage: digitisation, online accessibility and digital preservation: report on the implementation of Commission Recommendation 2011/711/EU*, http://ec.europa.eu/digital-agenda/en/news/european-commissions-report-digitisation-online-accessibility-and-digital-preservation-cultural.
5   See, for example, http://consumerist.com/2011/03/07/harper-collins-starts-charging-libraries-for-popular-e-books.

Orphan works

Chapter 6 covers:

6.1   Definition

'Orphan work' is the term that has come to be used to describe a work where the rights holder is difficult or even impossible to identify or locate. The orphan works problem tends to be more prevalent amongst older works, where the copyright term far exceeds the 'commercial' life of the work. It also tends to be the case that the less commercially successful a work has proved to be, the more administrative effort is required to search for possible authors. The IPO estimate that there are at least 91 million orphan works in the UK.[1]

As far as the CDPA 1988 is concerned, the meaning of orphan work is given in section 3 of Schedule ZA1:

3(1) . . . a relevant work is an orphan work if—

    (a)   there is a single rightholder in the work and the rightholder has not been identified or located, or

    (b)   there is more than one rightholder in the work and none of the rightholders has been identified or located, despite a diligent search for the rightholder or rightholders having been carried out and recorded in accordance with paragraph 5.

(2)   Subject as follows, a relevant work with more than one rightholder is also an orphan work for the purposes of this Schedule if—

> (a) one or more of the rightholders has been identified or located, and
>
> (b) one or more of the rightholders has not been identified or located despite a diligent search for the rightholder or rightholders having been carried out and recorded in accordance with paragraph 5.
>
> Source: The National Archives, 2015

Examples of orphan works can include the following:

- obscure works of literature or art
- copyright works coming to the end of their protection period
- anonymous or pseudonymous works
- works not traditionally published
- works no longer commercially published.

The orphan works issue is linked to the lack of appropriate attribution of authorship in many creative sectors. It is especially problematic in the area of visual art and photography.

There are a number of factors which can lead to a work being an orphan work:

1 When there is no information about the author on the work itself. Books and journals will normally have ISBNs and ISSNs, respectively, but for some types of material there won't be any markings along similar lines. It is highly likely that there won't be any information about the author on photographs, for example. In addition to ISBNs and ISSNs, there are a number of other identifier systems. They include:

- ISAN for audiovisual material
- ISMN for sheet music
- ISWC for musical scores
- ISRC for sound recordings
- EIDR, the entertainment identifier registry for films.

In addition there is the ISBD – international standard bibliographic description – which is useful for descriptions of bibliographic resources in any type of catalogue. It can relate to descriptions of books, maps, serials, sound recordings, computer files and other electric resources.
The structure of an ISBD record includes a section for the resource identifier (such as an ISBN or an ISSN).

2 The term of copyright is dependent upon the date of the death of the author. It isn't always easy to know when an author died, and therefore, to be able to calculate when the work comes out of copyright protection.

3 The author is known, but has died, and there is no information about his or her heirs.

4   The company that held the copyright no longer exists. Indeed the *Gowers Review* (HM Treasury, 2006) uses the word 'abandonware' to describe when businesses go bankrupt or merge, and where any information about copyright ownership gets lost.

5   The author is no longer the rights owner.

6.2   Legally compliant orphan works solutions

Since October 2014 there have been a number of legally compliant means of copying orphan works. The first of these is in the form of a copyright exception (CDPA 1988, section 44B), although this is only available for non-commercial use of orphan works by publicly accessible libraries, educational establishments, museums, archives, film or heritage institutions, and public service broadcasting organizations. The second solution is in the form of an orphan works licence. Both the copyright exception and the UK orphan works licensing scheme are designed to complement one another, but they are separate and distinct. Indeed, the first solution, in the form of a copyright exception can be traced back to the European Commission, whereas the second solution, in the form of a licensing scheme, derives from the UK government. The two solutions are compared in Table 6.1 on the next page.

6.2.1   The copyright exception for orphan works

The EU directive on orphan works 2012/28/EU is implemented in the UK through The Copyright and Rights in Performances (Certain Permitted Uses of Orphan Works) Regulations 2014 (SI 2014/2861). It inserts section 44B on 'Permitted uses of orphan works' into the CDPA 1988. Directive 2012/28/EU allows digitization of orphan works by certain cultural organizations. However:

- It only covers non-commercial use.
- It doesn't cover all types of copyright work (it is limited to written works, films, sound recordings, embedded works,[2] audiovisual works and sound recordings). It doesn't cover standalone images.
- There is no requirement to set aside money for absent rights holders.
- If the rights owners do reappear, compensation should be paid.[3]
- It requires a diligent search to be undertaken. The searcher must search the Office for Harmonization in the Internal Market (OHIM)[4] database (https://oami.europa.eu/orphanworks) to see if the work already appears on the database, and must provide OHIM with details of the diligent search for the rights holders which has been undertaken.
- It is possible to appeal to the Copyright Tribunal to determine a compensation amount in the event that the rights owner comes forward but where the relevant body and the rights owner have been unable to agree on a suitable figure.

Table 6.1 *Comparison of the copyright exception v. the IPO's orphan works licensing scheme*

	Copyright exception	Licence
Who is it for?	Publicly accessible libraries, educational establishments, museums, archives, film or audio heritage institutions, and public service broadcasting organizations.	Anyone.
What types of material does it cover?	Books, journals, newspapers, magazines or other writings which are in the collections of publicly accessible libraries, educational establishments, museums or archives; as well as cinematic or audiovisual works contained in the collections of film heritage institutions; and cinematographic, audio or audiovisual works produced by public service broadcasting organizations before 31 December 2002 and contained in their archives. Also covers embedded works.	All types of work.
What sorts of uses?	Non-commercial use.	Can cover commercial or non-commercial uses.
Is there a cost?	No.	Yes, and this consists of an application processing charge plus the licence fee.
What if the rights owner turns up?	Within a reasonable period the licence holder is required to provide compensation to the rights holder for their use of the work.	The licence continues for the remainder of its unexpired term or until the expiration of the notice period as set out in the licence. The authorizing body (the IPO) will pay to the rights holder a sum equal to the licence fee paid by the licensee.
How long does the permission to use the work last for?	Until copyright expires or until rights holder turns up, whichever is the sooner.	For up to seven years. Potentially this could be renewed for a further seven-year period.
Coverage	Across the member states of the EU.	UK only.
Requirements	A diligent search is required.	A diligent search is required. If the licence is renewed, then an updated diligent search needs to be carried out.

The exception is only for the benefit of certain types of cultural institution:

- publicly accessible libraries
- educational establishments
- museums

- archives
- film or heritage institutions
- public service broadcasting organizations.

The institutions covered by the directive are only permitted to use the orphan works in order to achieve the aims of their public interest missions – notably preservation, restoration and the provision of cultural and educational access to works contained in their collections. These organizations can:

- make an orphan work available to the public
- reproduce an orphan work for digitization purposes
- index, catalogue, preserve and restore an orphan work.

The main purpose of the directive is to create a legal framework to ensure the lawful, cross-border online access to orphan works contained in online digital libraries or archives operated by a variety of institutions in pursuance of the public interest mission of those institutions. The aim of the directive is for there to be a system of mutual recognition of the orphan status of a work throughout the EU, thus obviating the need for multiple diligent searches. This approach allows libraries and other beneficiaries to enjoy legal certainty as to the 'orphan status' of a particular work. In order to establish that a work has 'orphan' status, libraries, educational establishments, museums or archives, film heritage institutions and public service broadcasting organizations are required to carry out a prior diligent search in the member state where the work was first published.

6.2.2   Orphan works licences

6.2.2.1   Introduction
Before applying for a licence to copy an orphan work ask yourself:

1 Is it likely that the work is still in copyright?
2 Does my intended use fall within one of the copyright exceptions?
3 Is there a non-orphan work that I could use instead?
4 Could I commission a new work?

6.2.2.2   IPO licensing of orphan works
Details of the orphan works licensing scheme are available at www.gov.uk/apply-for-a-licence-to-use-an-orphan-work. The scheme:

- is administered by the UK IPO www.gov.uk/ipo

- uses an electronic application system

★ - uses a searchable register of the licences granted,
    www.orphanworkslicensing.service.gov.uk/view-register.

The IPO's role as the authorizing body (in place of the absent rights holder) is to:

- consider applications to use works
- determine licence fees
- grant licences to use works
- hold monies for a specified period.

6.2.2.3   Features of the orphan works licences

- They apply only for use within the UK.
- They can be for either commercial or non-commercial use.
- They are non-exclusive. There is a statutory prohibition against the grant of exclusive licences.
- They can last for up to seven years.
- A diligent search must be undertaken.
- It will be possible to renew them (but this requires an updated diligent search).
- They cover all types of works.
- Sub-licensing is not permitted.
- The licence may be granted subject to conditions.
- The IPO has the discretion to vary the licence terms during its term.

Orphan works licences are not freely transferrable. However, the IPO as the authorizing body may allow licence transfer where there are compelling reasons to do so.

6.2.2.4   Licence application

Applicants must provide information in the orphan licence application form showing that a diligent search for the rights holders in the work has been conducted, and specifying how they intend to use the orphan work.

The applicant will also need:

- a debit or credit card to pay the application fee, payable at the time of submitting their application and, if the licence application is approved, they will later need their payment card in order to pay the licence fee
- information about the work, including the title, if there is one, as well as a description of the work, along with details of whether it has been previously published and information about its provenance (i.e. how the applicant came by the work)

- any information they have about right holders
- if the work is a photograph or other piece of still visual art, an image to upload.

The licence application can only be completed online. There is no other means of submitting an application, such as by letter.

The IPO will consider licence applications as quickly as possible and they will normally aim to have made a decision within ten working days. This may not always be possible if the application is a complex one or involves numerous different works with multiple right holders. Once it has reached its decision on whether or not to issue a licence, it will e-mail the decision to the applicant. If the licence application has been rejected, either in part or in its entirety, then the IPO will provide the applicant with the reasons for reaching that decision. There is detailed guidance available in IPO ✱ (2014) *Orphan Works Licensing Scheme Overview for Applicants,* www.gov.uk/government/ uploads/system/uploads/attachment_data/file/368417/orphan-applicants.pdf.

6.2.2.5   Orphan works licence costs

The cost of obtaining a licence consists of two separate and distinct charges. The first of these is an application fee, which is the fee paid to cover the administrative costs of processing the licence application. This fee is payable at the time when the licence application is submitted. It is non-refundable, regardless of whether or not the licence application is approved. The second cost component is the fee to cover the cost of the licence itself, and this will depend upon the nature of the work and the use that is being licensed. The IPO is entitled to charge a *'reasonable* licence fee' for the licence term and it has worked closely with sector-specific groups in order to ascertain potential licence fees as well as looking at the prices charged for using similar non-orphan works in the same way. The payments due to the IPO are summarized in Table 6.2 on the next page.

The licence fee is held by the IPO in a ring-fenced account on behalf of the absent rights holder, should they later come forward. The IPO are required to retain these fees for at least eight years from the date on which the licence was granted. After eight years, if no rights holder comes forward to claim ownership, the IPO can deduct its reasonable costs from the retained fee, and apply any surplus 'to fund social, cultural and educational activities'. If a rights holder comes forward within eight years from the date of the licence grant and satisfies the proof of ownership requirements of the orphan work, the IPO must pay the rights holder within two months the licence fee paid by the orphan licensee.

Regulation 12 of SI 2014/2863 states that:

(2) If the authorising body has verified the diligent search but has not granted an orphan licence then the work shall, to the extent of the rights of the identified right holder, cease to be an orphan work.

Table 6.2 *Payments due to the IPO on orphan works licences*

	Application fee	**Licence fee**
Method of payment	Credit or debit card using a secure payment process.	Credit or debit card using a secure payment process.
When payment is made	At the time of submitting the licence application.	Once the licence application has been approved, prior to the licence being issued.
Amount	The fee structure is tiered with a charge for one item set at £20, or up to 30 items within the same application, where the cost for 30 items is £80.	Depends on the nature of the use(s)[5] being licensed. The cost for licensing an image for non-commercial use is 10 pence. Once you have selected the type of work that you want to use and the types of use(s) that you wish the licence to cover, the licence fee will be displayed.[6]

(3)   If the authorising body has granted an orphan licence then the orphan licence shall continue for the remainder of its unexpired term or until the expiration of the notice period

Source: The National Archives, 2014

If the rights holder comes forward after the eight-year period, the IPO has the discretion to remunerate the rights holder as it considers reasonable in all the circumstances.

6.2.2.6   Commercial v. non-commercial use
Non-commercial use

If you apply for a licence to cover 'non-commercial' use of an orphan work, you will be able to use that work for any of the uses listed below as long as the circumstances of your particular use are non-commercial.

* free handouts for a live event, exhibition or similar
* use in a live event, exhibition or similar
* in a newsletter, bulletin, e-newsletter or e-bulletin
* in non-commercial promotional material – print and digital
* digitized and made available online, including on social media
* preservation purposes
* use on stage or in performance
* educational purposes – use in learning/ training materials, including e-learning
* use in a thesis/dissertation
* personal use.

The licence fee for non-commercial use is significantly lower than for commercial use, with a set licence fee of 10 pence per work for all non-commercial uses.

Commercial use

'Commercial use' covers any uses either by individuals or by organizations which make money from the work such as selling copies of the work or directly charging for access. The use would be deemed to be commercial whether any charges were intended to make a profit or merely to cover costs.

As well as activities that generate revenue, such as merchandizing or selling copies of a publication, commercial use would also cover any other uses that are commercial in nature, such as any use in commercial advertising, marketing or promotion activities. Where the use was to promote a free exhibition of which the work was a part, this would not be commercial use, whereas the use of an orphan work, such as a photograph on a poster, to promote or market an exhibition where there was a charge, would be commercial.

When considering whether a particular use is commercial or not, what matters is whether the use itself is thought to be commercial (where it is aimed at making a profit from the use of the work). It is irrelevant whether or not the applicant is a not-for-profit organization.

6.2.2.7   Orphan works register

The IPO maintains an orphan works register: www.orphanworkslicensing. ✷ service.gov.uk/view-register. It contains details of:

- applications for orphan works licences
- licences that have been granted
- applications that have been refused.

The register can be used by rights holders wishing to check whether any of their works are being considered as potential orphans or have been licensed for use after the diligent search. However, the onus for finding rights holders is on the potential licensee. The following information is displayed on the register:

- organization name
- application number
- application date
- use
- status of application
- title or short description
- full description

- category
- type of work
- missing right holders
- known identifiers
- known rights holders
- where work held
- located rights holders
- publication or broadcast dates.

The IPO as the authorizing body is required to make the register available to the public by electronic means and free of charge.

6.2.2.8   Reasons why an orphan works licence may be refused

A licence may be refused:

- where the diligent search is inadequate
- where the IPO considers that the proposed adaptation or use of the work is not appropriate
- where it would not be in the public interest to grant a licence for that use.

The IPO also has a wide discretion to refuse to grant a licence on 'any other reasonable ground'.

In the case of adaptation this would be relevant where the use involves addition, modification or deletion to the work. It might, for example, involve resizing or cropping a photograph, or recolouring an artwork and the use might potentially be deemed to be a derogatory use of the work. In the case of inappropriate use this would cover where the use might be seen as offensive, in poor taste or contentious, having regard to the circumstances of the case.

6.2.2.9   Complaints and appeals

A rights holder has a right of appeal to the First-tier Tribunal where it considers that the IPO has acted improperly or failed to comply with its obligations under the regulations. An orphan licensee can appeal to the Copyright Tribunal (whose rules of procedure can be found at www.ipo.gov.uk/ctribunal/ctribunal-application/ctribunal-application-procedure.htm) on a number of grounds:

- if the IPO refuses to grant a licence
- because of any conditions imposed by the IPO in connection with the licence that has been granted
- in respect of the licence fee amount.

If someone is unhappy with the final response to their complaint and it's not something that can be appealed to the Copyright Tribunal or the First-tier Tribunal, they can refer their complaint to the Parliamentary and Health Service Ombudsman.

6.2.2.10   Extended collective licensing

The collecting societies represent particular groups of rights holders, from whom they have been given a mandate. The problem with orphan works is that, by their very nature, there is no one around to give the collecting society such a mandate. Extended collective licensing is a way of solving this problem, because it means that where a collecting society covers a category of works such as – but not limited to – the authors and publishers of book and journal articles, they are then able to apply to the Secretary of State for the ability to represent all rights owners of that type of material, unless the rights owner comes forward and says that they do not want to be represented by that collecting society. In this way a licence can be issued for the use of orphan works by a collecting society, even though they haven't been given a mandate directly from the rights holder in the orphan work.

The Secretary of State can authorize licensing bodies to operate an extended collective licensing scheme. The authorization is for a period of up to five years and it could be issued subject to conditions.

- The authorization will specify the *relevant works* to which it applies and the *permitted use*.
- The authorized body will already license content within that category of work and have significant representation within it.
- It must have adequate opt-out arrangements.
- It must have appropriate means for publicizing the scheme, and for contacting non-member rights holders.
- It will have the informed consent of a substantial proportion of its members to the proposed extended collective licensing scheme.
- It will be required to operate in accordance with its code of practice.

Collecting societies that have been authorized to operate an extended collective licensing scheme:

- will issue non-exclusive licences
- will charge an administration fee or 'processing charge' within the overall licence cost which goes towards the general costs of the licensing society
- will distribute monies from the licence fee to rights holders.

In order to pave the way for extended collective licensing schemes, legislation was required in order to exonerate organizations offering a scheme from civil and, potentially, criminal liability:

- Section 77 of the Enterprise and Regulatory Reform Act 2013 inserts sections 116A–116D into the CDPA 1988 covering orphan works licensing and extended collective licensing.
- SI 2014/2588: The Copyright (Extended Collective Licensing) Regulations facilitates the setting up of extended licensing schemes operated by the collective licensing societies which would permit uses of orphan works that would otherwise infringe.

Retention and application of undistributed licence fees

Where the rights owners haven't been located after three years, the licensing society must pass the net licence fee (after their administration costs) to the designated account of the Secretary of State. This is subject to regulation 19(2), where the Secretary of State could direct the licensing body to retain the licence fee in a designated account for a specific period after the expiration of the initial three year period, and they would then be required to transfer the licence fee to the Secretary of State at the end of that period. Regulation 19 of SI 2014/2588 deals with retention and application of undistributed licence fees. Regulation 19(3) says:

> The Secretary of State must retain any net licence fee, which has not been distributed by the relevant licensing body, for a period of 8 years from the date of authorisation of the Extended Collective Licensing Scheme and may then determine the use of the net licence fee, including, by applying some or all of the net licence fee to fund social, cultural and educational activities for the benefit of non-member right holders.
>
> Source: The National Archives, 2014

6.3   Diligent search

All of the legal solutions for copying orphan works – the copyright exception in s 44B of the CDPA 1988, the licences available from the IPO or the orphan works licences from collecting societies authorized by the IPO to operate such a licence – require a diligent search to be undertaken.

It is important that a thorough search is completed, and that there is recorded evidence of the diligent search having been made. Indeed, one of the reasons why an orphan works licence application may be refused is lack of the necessary evidence to show that an adequate diligent search has been undertaken. Where someone applies to the IPO for a licence, the IPO has a responsibility to satisfy itself as to the quality of the diligent search undertaken before a licence can be issued. It must ensure that the search has been carried out in good faith and that the appropriate sources for the category of work in question have been consulted.

The IPO has produced guidance and checklists to help people complete a ★ diligent search. It covers separate guidance for diligent searches relating to film and sound, for literary works, and for still visual art. The guidance can be found at www.gov.uk/government/publications/orphan-works-diligent-search-guidance-for-applicants and is summarized in Figure 6.1.

Film and sound	Literary works	Still visual art
Includes • Films • TV programmes • Amateur film footage • Music sound recordings • Non-music sound recordings (such as interviews)	Includes • Fiction books • Non-fiction books • Manuscripts • Essays • Letters • Diaries • Short stories • Notes • Poems • Dramatic works such as scripts, plays and screenplays	Includes • Photographs • Pictures • Paintings • Posters • Sketches • Drawings • Etchings • Cartoons • Sculptures

Figure 6.1 *Guidance on diligent search available from the IPO*

A few key points about undertaking a diligent search are given below. For more specific information, it is worth noting that the IPO has produced detailed guidance[7] on undertaking a diligent search for specific categories of works (film and sound; literary works; still visual art). This reflects the fact that different categories of material will require a different mix of sources to be checked as part of the diligent search:

- A 'reasonable search' of the 'relevant sources' must be conducted. The regulation requires applicants to search the register maintained by the UK IPO and the relevant databases maintained by the Office for Harmonization in the Internal Market (OHIM); and
- Where the UK IPO and OHIM searches fail to reveal the owner of the work, applicants must then check the sources listed in Part 2 of Schedule ZA1 to the CDPA ('Sources to be searched during diligent search'): these are set out in the Certain Permitted Uses of Orphan Works Regulations (SI 2014/2861), and different sources (including collecting societies) are listed, depending on the type of work in question, e.g. audiovisual, visual works, newspapers, etc.
- If there is evidence to suggest that relevant information on rights holders is to be found in other countries, a relevant body carrying out a search must also consult the sources of information available in those other countries.
- A diligent search will be valid for seven years.

The sources appropriate for each category of works are determined by each member state but they must include as a minimum the sources listed in the annex to the directive (2012/28/EU). In the UK the sources to be searched during a diligent search are listed in Schedule ZA1, Part 2 of SI 2014/2861: The Copyright and Rights in Performances (Certain Permitted Uses of Orphan Works) Regulations (see Figure 6.2).

---

1. Published books
   (a) legal deposit, library catalogues and authority files maintained by libraries and other institutions;
   (b) the publishers' and authors' associations in the country in question;
   (c) existing databases and registries, WATCH (Writers, Artists and their Copyright Holders), the ISBN (International Standard Book Number) and databases listing books in print;
   (d) the databases of the relevant collecting societies, including reproduction rights organizations;
   (e) sources that integrate multiple databases and registries, including VIAF (Virtual International Authority Files) and ARROW (Accessible Registries of Rights Information and Orphan Works).

2. Newspapers, magazines, journals and periodicals
   (a) the ISSN (International Standard Serial Number) for periodical publications;
   (b) indexes and catalogues from library holdings and collections;
   (c) legal deposit;
   (d) the publishers' associations and the authors' and journalists' associations in the country in question;
   (e) the databases of relevant collecting societies including reproduction rights organizations.

3. Visual works, including fine art, photography, illustration, design, architecture, sketches of the latter works and other such works that are contained in books, journals, newspapers and magazines or other works
   (a) the sources referred to in paragraphs 1 and 2;
   (b) the databases of the relevant collecting societies, in particular for visual arts, and including reproduction rights organizations;
   (c) the databases of picture agencies, where applicable.

4. Audiovisual works and sound recordings
   (a) legal deposit;
   (b) the producers' associations in the country in question;
   (c) databases of film or audio heritage institutions and national libraries;
   (d) databases with relevant standards and identifiers such as ISAN (International Standard Audiovisual Number) for audiovisual material, ISWC (International Standard Music Work Code) for musical works and ISRC (International Standard Recording Code) for sound recordings;
   (e) the databases of the relevant collecting societies, in particular for authors, performers, sound recording producers and audiovisual producers;
   (f) credits and other information appearing on the work's packaging;
   (g) databases of other relevant associations representing a specific category of rightholders.

5. Relevant works which have not been published or broadcast
Those sources that are listed in paragraphs 1 to 4 above which are appropriate to a relevant work which is unpublished.

Figure 6.2 *Sources to be searched listed for each type of work (Source: Schedule ZA1, Part 2 of SI 2014/2861)*

If there is an existing diligent search for the rights holder in the work a licence applicant wishes to use, they are able to rely on that search without having to conduct a new search, provided that it:

- was submitted with a previous, successful, licence application up to seven years ago; or
- was carried out under the EU Directive with the details published on the OHIM database.

Notes

1   *UK Opens Access to 91 Million Orphan Works*, IPO press release, 29 October 2014.
2   A copyright-protected work may include other works within it. If, for example, a book includes photographs, these will have their own separate rights. Standalone photographs and other images are not currently within the scope of the directive, but the directive would cover such items if they were embedded within other copyright works.
3   As this is a copyright exception, no money will have been paid to cover the use of the work. The regulations (SI 2014/2861 regulation 7) say:

> (3) A relevant body that is using or has used the orphan work must within a reasonable period provide the rightholder with fair compensation for that body's use of the relevant work together with information on how the fair compensation has been calculated.
> (4) If a relevant body and the rightholder cannot agree on the amount of compensation payable, either of them may apply to the Copyright Tribunal to determine the amount.

Source: The National Archives, 2014

4   The Office for Harmonization in the Internal Market is the European Union agency responsible for managing the Community trade mark and the registered Community design; and following the coming into force of the Orphan Works Directive 2012/28/EU it is responsible for establishing and managing the European database containing information about orphan works.
5   A licence applicant can apply for more than one use for the same work within a single licence application, but will need to bear in mind that each separate use will incur its own licence fee. Regulation 10(1)(a) of SI 2014/2863 says that the charge made to the orphan licensee should be a *reasonable* licence fee for the period of the licence and that this will be calculated with regard to relevant factors, which shall include the level of

licence fees which are achieved under licences for a similar use of similar
relevant works which are not orphan works.

6 In a small number of cases, the licence fee will be set on a 'price on
application' basis, which means the applicant will be asked to e-mail the
IPO, which will then provide a licence fee for that type of work and use.

7 Orphan works diligent search guidance for applicants (IPO, 2014),
https://www.gov.uk/government/publications/orphan-works-diligent-search-
guidance-for-applicants.

Copyright compliance

Chapter 7 covers:

7.1   Introduction

In order for library and information professionals to ensure compliance with copyright law, it is obviously a prerequisite that they are as clear as they can be about what would constitute an infringement of copyright. Copyright infringements can be divided into two categories – primary and secondary infringements. The chapter considers what constitutes an infringement of copyright, and its potential consequences.

It is worth thinking of copyright issues and questions in terms of risk management, rather than expecting all copying scenarios to have unambiguous and clear-cut black-and-white answers. The chapter explores what might be thought to be low, medium and high risks, and what steps can be taken to reduce or minimize those risks. It also looks at what happens if or when things do go wrong, using a number of case studies and the terms of the settlement in each case, and considers the various options available for settling disputes, whether formally or informally.

Another issue addressed in the chapter is that of who might be held to be liable for an infringement of copyright, and this is done from the perspective of a number of different stakeholders – library users, libraries, directors, intermediary service providers, employers and employees.

As well as thinking of copyright compliance as a matter of legal observance, the chapter also considers it from the perspective of it being a matter of professional ethics.

Figure 7.1 sets out some key steps that libraries can take to ensure compliance in its dealings with copyright material.

For all types of libraries:

- Place copyright notices and/or posters next to all public access computers and photocopiers.
- Familiarize yourself with the terms of your licence agreements, and ensure compliance with those terms.
- Have a formal written policy on intellectual property rights in the staff handbook. Draw this to the attention of staff where appropriate (such as when the copyright policy is updated, or when new staff join).
- Provide regular training and awareness sessions covering copyright law, with guidance as to what is and what is not acceptable.
- Have a central point for copyright queries so that people who are unsure as to what is allowed know where to go to get assistance, and ensure that this is well publicized.
- Don't override DRM systems.
- Don't remove rights management information from digital works.

For publicly accessible libraries:

- Keep declaration forms for six years plus the current year.

Figure 7.1 *Steps towards copyright compliance*

The chapter concludes by looking at the copyright clearance process, from tracing the rights owner through to getting their written permission to do the particular type of copying for which you are seeking authorization.

7.2   Infringement

Copyright infringement takes place where someone uses either the whole or a substantial part of a work without the rights holders' permission (whether that is achieved by having their direct permission, or indirectly by having a licence with a collective management organization mandated by the rights holder to act on their behalf) and where none of the copyright exceptions applies.

It is difficult to be prescriptive about where the line should be drawn, because although the term 'substantial part' is used in the CDPA 1988 it is not defined within the legislation. We have to turn to case law for guidance; and that is of limited value because every case will be different. It isn't simply a question of quantity – how much of a work or what percentage has been copied. The phrase 'substantial part' has been interpreted by the courts to mean a *qualitatively significant* part of a work even where this is not a large part of the overall work. In other words, an infringement can take place even if the amount taken wasn't large in terms of quantity, as illustrated by the examples given in Figure 7.2.

Examples from court cases of what were considered to be a 'substantial part' of a work:

- Eleven-word extracts from newspaper articles can infringe copyright (CJEU judgment in Infopaq International v Dankse Dagblades Forening case C-5/08).
- An extract of 250 words from James Joyce's *Ulysses*, which represented less than 1/1000th of the work (Sweeney v Macmillan Publishers Ltd 2001 EWHC Ch 460 22nd November 2001). They were substantial because their inclusion made the text original and distinct.
- Four lines of a 32-line poem (Kipling v Genatosan (1923) MacG Cop Cas (1923-28) 203). The lines in Kipling's poem *If* were important lines because they formed an essential part of the crescendo in the poem.
- Fifty-four lines from a computer program which constituted 0.03% of the program (Veritas Operating Corporation v Microsoft Corporation, 562 F. Supp. 2d 1141 Dist. Court, WD Washington 2008).
- Thirty seconds from an hour-long interview (Pro Sieben Media AG v Carlton UK Television Ltd [1998] EWCA Civ 2001 (17 December 1998)). The Pro Sieben logo was displayed on the clip although there was no acknowledgement of their ownership of the copyright.
- Sampling of 3 notes (less than 2 seconds) of a guitar solo (Bridgeport Music Inc. v Dimension Films 2005 410 F. 3d 792 (6th Cir. 2005)).

Figure 7.2 *What is 'substantial'?*

The question of what constitutes a 'substantial part' has to be considered on a case-by-case basis, because every situation will have its own unique combination of facts – and because it isn't simply a question of amount or quantity. It is precisely for these reasons that one cannot come up with a set of 'safe copying guidelines'. CILIP's copyright poster (www.cilip.org.uk/cilip/advocacy-campaigns-awards/ advocacy-campaigns/copyright/briefings-resources/copyright-poster) simply states that the amount copied must be both fair and justifiable, although the accompanying guidance does say that '5% of a published work could possibly be reasonable'.

7.2.1 Primary infringement

Section 16 of the CDPA 1988 lists a series of rights which are exclusive to the owner of the copyright in the work. They are the rights:

- to copy the work
- to issue copies of the work to the public

- to rent or lend the work to the public
- to perform, show or play the work in public
- to communicate the work to the public
- to make an adaptation of the work or do any of the above in relation to an adaptation.

To do any of these activities without authorization would be a primary infringement of copyright. 'Authorization' doesn't necessarily mean getting the direct permission of the copyright owner. It could, for example, be that one of the statutory exceptions provides the required authorization or that you have a licence agreement in place from a collective licensing society mandated by the rights owner to act on their behalf, where that licence covers your intended use of the work.

7.2.2   Secondary infringement

In addition to the primary infringements listed in Section 7.2.1, there are a number of activities which would constitute a secondary infringement of copyright. Sections 22–26 of the CDPA 1988 list activities which constitute secondary infringements of copyright. They are:

- importing an infringing copy
- possessing or dealing with an infringing copy
- providing the means for making infringing copies
- permitting use of premises for infringing performance
- provision of apparatus for infringing performance, etc.

7.2.3   Other offences

It is illegal for someone to circumvent a digital rights management system or to tell others how to circumvent such a system, for example:

- if you knew how to download and convert video files on the BBC iPlayer into DRM free files which don't expire
- if you knew how to get around a newspaper website's paywall and were tempted to tell other people how to do this so that they could deliberately avoid buying a digital subscription.

Another offence relates to rights management information. Anyone who knowingly and without authority removes or alters electronic rights management information can be taken to court by the copyright holder. Section 296 ZG (7) of the CDPA 1988 defines 'rights management information' as being any information provided by the copyright owner or the holder of any right under copyright which identifies the work, the author, the copyright owner or the holder of any intellectual property rights, or information about the terms and conditions of use of the work, and any numbers or codes that represent such information.

Source: The National Archives, 2015

This offence can be traced back to Article 12 of the WIPO Copyright Treaty 1996, which sets out obligations concerning rights management information, including the requirement for contracting parties to provide effective legal remedies against people who remove or alter rights management information without authority. Don't remove rights management information from digital works, for example:

- if you know how to remove a header appearing on every page of a pdf document which identifies the author of the work
- if you know how to remove the metadata associated with a digital image which contains information such as a copyright notice and credits.

7.2.4 Remedies

The remedies available for copyright infringement include:

- account of profits
- damages
- injunctions
- undertaking to take a licence
- an order for the delivery up of the infringing copies (under section 99 of the CDPA), although a time limit of six years from the date on which the infringing copy or illicit recording was made is stipulated in sections 113 and 203 respectively of the CDPA, in line with the Limitation Act 1980
- the right to seize infringing copies.

7.2.4.1 Account of profits

An account of profits is an equitable remedy used against a defendant to recover the profits that they made as a result of their wrongful actions. It may not be easy to determine in practice because it will involve examining the defendant's accounting record in order to work out what portion of their gross profits were derived from their wrongful actions.

7.2.4.2 Damages

In English law a successful claimant is entitled to either an account of profits or damages to compensate for their loss. Section 97 of the CDPA 1988 says:

97 Provisions as to damages in infringement action

(1) Where in an action for infringement of copyright it is shown that at the time of the infringement the defendant did not know, and had no reason to believe, that copyright subsisted in the work to which the action relates, the plaintiff is not entitled to damages against him, but without prejudice to any other remedy.
(2) The court may in an action for infringement of copyright having regard to all the circumstances, and in particular to –

(a) the flagrancy of the infringement, and
(b) any benefit accruing to the defendant by reason of the infringement,

award such additional damages as the justice of the case may require.

Source: The National Archives, 2015

In David Hoffman v Drug Abuse Resistance Education (UK) Limited [2012] EWPCC 2, Judge Birss QC found that the defendant had committed acts restricted by copyright, specifically the act of communicating the work to the public, which thereby infringed Mr Hoffman's copyright. He ordered for £10,000 in damages and £2,444.57 in interest to be paid to Mr Hoffman.

7.2.4.3   Injunctions

An injunction is an equitable remedy. It is a court order which requires the party on whom the injunction is served either to do or to refrain from doing certain acts. By way of example, in 2002 the Copyright Licensing Agency successfully obtained a High Court injunction, seizing over 500 illegally copied books from a copyshop in Nottingham.

7.2.4.4   Undertaking to take a licence (of right)

This remedy relates to where there has been a report of the Competition Commission (The Competition Commission closed on 1 April 2014. Its functions have transferred to the Competition and Markets Authority (CMA)), for example where there has been a refusal of a copyright owner to grant licences on reasonable terms. The defendant undertakes to take a licence on such terms as may be agreed, or, if no agreement is reached, where the matter is settled before the Copyright Tribunal.

7.2.4.5   Right to seize infringing copies

In section 100 of the CDPA 1988 there is a right to seize infringing copies and other articles, and in section 196 there is a right to seize illicit recordings. The right to seize and detain is exercisable subject to any decision of the court (under section 114), and is also subject to a number of conditions:

- Before anything is seized under section 100, notice of the time and place of the proposed seizure must be given to a local police station.
- A person may for the purpose of exercising the right conferred by section 100 enter premises to which the public have access but may not seize anything in the possession, custody or control of a person at a permanent or regular place of business of his, and may not use any force.
- At the time when anything is seized under this section there shall be left at the place where it was seized a notice in a form prescribed by the Secretary of State.

7.2.5   Norwich Pharmacal Orders

A Norwich Pharmacal order is a device which can be used to find out the identity of, amongst other things, copyright infringers. The name derives from a House of Lords decision in the case of Norwich Pharmacal Co v Customs and Excise Commissioners [1974] AC 133). This established the doctrine that a party to potential litigation could seek disclosure of information held by a third party which might identify others against whom a claim could be made.

When a court grants an application for a Norwich Pharmacal order, the order then requires the disclosure of information to a requesting party when it can be shown that the party seeking relief would find it helpful in identifying those against whom a claim could be made, which would be useful to a party seeking relief in cases such as the infringement of intellectual property rights.

In a case of online copyright infringement it means in practice that an internet service provider could be required through a court order to disclose the details of customer(s) who have downloaded infringing copies of content. It does not necessarily mean that all of those who are identified as a result of the process are then pursued through the courts. Potentially, a Norwich Pharmacal Order could be used merely as a way of obtaining a long list of people who are then sent letters demanding recompense for the alleged infringement(s). This has been referred to as speculative invoicing or as 'pay up or else' schemes.[1]

One example of where a Norwich Pharmacal order was used in order to establish the identity of copyright infringers was the legal case Golden Eye (International) Limited v Telefonica UK Limited [2012] EWHC 723 (Ch) - where the High Court made an order against O_2 (the sixth largest ISP in the UK) in favour of a number of owners of copyright in pornographic films.

Another example of where a Norwich Pharmacal Order was applied for was in the case of G and G v Wikimedia [2009] EWHC 3148 (QB). In this case, a mother sought an order to require Wikimedia to disclose the IP address of a person in order to identify them as she was seeking legal remedies to prevent any further breach of privacy or disclosure of confidential information. The person in question had amended an article on Wikipedia and inserted private and sensitive information in relation to her and her child. At the end of the hearing Mr Justice Tugendhat made the order that the respondent disclose the IP information.

When a judge considers an application for a Norwich Pharmacal Order in a copyright infringement case they would look at the proportionality of the proposed order. It would mean consideration of the balance of the interests of the claimants against the interests of the intended defendants. Would the copyright holder's interests in enforcing their copyrights outweigh the defendants' interest in protecting their privacy and data protection rights?

And the ruling can place conditions on the use of the Norwich Pharmacal Order. For example, in the Golden Eye case, the order was made on the condition that the order and the proposed letter of claim to be distributed to the intended defendants was properly framed so as to safeguard their legitimate interests – most notably the interests of those who might have been erroneously identified as infringers.

7.2.6 Website blocking

Copyright holders have sought to block access to websites and streaming services which facilitate copyright infringement. This has been achieved through the use of court orders or takedown notices. Examples of where this has been done include:

- The Pirate Bay (Dramatico Entertainment Ltd v British Sky Broadcasting Ltd [2012] EWHC 268 (Ch))
- FirstRow Sports (The Football Association Premier League Ltd v British Sky Broadcasting Ltd & Ors [2013] EWHC 2058 (Ch) (16 July 2013))
- RnbXclusive (shut down by the Serious Organised Crime Agency)
- Kickass Torrents, Fenopy and H33t (EMI Records Ltd & Ors v British Sky Broadcasting Ltd & Ors [2013] EWHC 379 (Ch))
- Newzbin 2 (Twentieth Century Fox Film Corporation v British Telecommunications plc [2011] EWHC 1981 (Ch))
- TubePlus and SolarMovie (Paramount Home Entertainment International Ltd and others v British Sky Broadcasting Ltd and others [2013] EWHC 3479 (Ch))

The legislative authority used in UK cases where a court injunction is being applied for is s 97A of the CDPA 1988:

(1) The High Court (in Scotland, the Court of Session) shall have power to grant an injunction against a service provider, where that service provider has actual knowledge of another person using their service to infringe copyright.

(2) In determining whether a service provider has actual knowledge for the purpose of this section, a court shall take into account all matters which appear to it in the particular circumstances to be relevant and, amongst other things, shall have regard to—

    (a) whether a service provider has received a notice through a means of contact made available in accordance with regulation 6(1)(c) of the Electronic Commerce (EC Directive) Regulations 2002 (SI 2002/2013); and

    (b) the extent to which any notice includes—

        (i) the full name and address of the sender of the notice;

        (ii) details of the infringement in question.

(3) In this section "service provider" has the meaning given to it by regulation 2 of the Electronic Commerce (EC Directive) Regulations 2002.

Source: The National Archives, 2014

The Open Rights Group maintains a list of sites that have been subjected to blocking: https://wiki.openrightsgroup.org/wiki/Website_blocking.

There is a danger of accidental blocking or overblocking, as happened to the *Radio Times* website, which inadvertently got caught up in the Premier League's battle against an infringing site (see Leo Kelion, Radio Times Caught up in Premier League's Piracy Site, *BBC News Online*, 14 August 2013).

In the CJEU judgment in UPC Telekabel Wien GmbH v Constantin Film Verleih GmbH und Wega Filmproduktionsgesellschaft GmbH (C-314/12) the court held that an internet service provider may be ordered to block its customers' access to a copyright-infringing website. The court found that an ISP such as UPC Telekabel which allows its customers to access protected subject-matter made available to the public on the internet by a third party is an intermediary whose services are used to infringe copyright. It isn't necessary to prove a relationship between the ISP and the infringing website, nor is it necessary to prove that customers of the ISP have accessed the infringing website.

A number of earlier legal cases had already established that internet providers can be regarded as intermediaries against whom such injunctions can be granted (see C-557/07 LSG-Gesellschaft zur Wahrnehmung von Leistungsschutzrechten and Case C-70/10 Scarlett Extended SA v SABAM). In the Scarlett v SABAM case, the court found that national courts cannot impose injunctions requiring ISPs to install filtering systems with a view to preventing the illegal downloading of sites. Rights holders can apply for injunctions against intermediaries such as ISPs whose services are being used by a third party to infringe their rights. But the court said that national authorities must not adopt measures requiring the carrying out of general monitoring of the information transmitted on its network, as that wasn't compatible with the E-Commerce Directive. The court was thinking here of where the filtering was applied indiscriminately to all of its customers as a preventative measure, where this was at the expense of the ISP/intermediary, and was in place for an unlimited period of time.

7.2.7 Differences between civil and criminal copyright cases

Copyright cases can be treated as a civil matter or as a criminal matter. Table 7.1 summarizes the differences. In order for a copyright infringement to be treated as a criminal matter it would normally involve actual knowledge, where the person doing the copying knew full well that they were breaking copyright law. *Mens rea* is a Latin term for 'guilty mind', where someone offends deliberately and knowingly. Another characteristic of criminal cases would be where the copying was being done on a commercial or industrial scale. Criminal intellectual property offences could be taking place within the workplace. Examples include:

Table 7.1 *Civil and criminal copyright cases*

	Civil	Criminal
Is knowledge required?	In a civil case, an individual could potentially infringe copyright without realizing that they had done so. But ignorance is no defence. Where the infringer did not know and had no reason to believe that copyright subsisted in the work, the rights owner cannot claim damages.	In a criminal case, it would involve actual knowledge (the legislation uses phrases such as 'knows or has reasons to believe'). Section 107 and 198 offences require criminal intent. The infringing activity has been undertaken deliberately. Examples can involve the making of pirate or counterfeit copies of CDs and DVDs, and their sale or distribution. There is a concept of *mens rea* or 'guilty mind' – where the infringement was undertaken intentionally or deliberately.
Scale of the infringing activity	The infringing activity may well have occurred on a small scale.	The infringing activity will be on an industrial or a commercial scale.
The penalties that are available[2]	The IPEC small claims track can be used for claims of less than £10,000 in damages. The IPEC multi-track can be used for claims of no more than £500,000 in damages and no more than £50,000 in legal costs. The Chancery Division of the High Court of England and Wales can be used for claims of over £500,000 in damages.[3]	Prison sentence of up to 10 years and/or a fine. In some cases the fine can be unlimited. In some cases the jail sentence can be 3 months or 6 months; or on indictment could be 2 years or 10 years. It depends on the offence. The IPO maintains a list of the penalties at www.gov.uk/government/publications/intellectual-property-offences.

Table 7.1 Continued	Civil	Criminal
Offences committed	Civil actions would be brought where either the whole or a substantial part of a work has been copied without authorization (see CDPA 1988 section 16(3)(a)).	Offences under: s 107 Criminal liability for making or dealing with infringing articles, etc. s 198 Criminal liability for making, dealing with or using illicit recordings The Fraud Act 2006 also contains offences of making or possessing articles for use in or in connection with fraud, and making or supplying articles for use in fraud.
Court	There are a number of courts which hear civil cases: County Court High Court (Chancery Division) Court of Appeal (Civil Division) Supreme Court European Court of Justice (where it relates to the interpretation of legislation derived from European Directives and Regulations). There is also the Intellectual Property Enterprise Court (IPEC – previously the Patents County Court). In the case of IPEC there is a damages cap of up to £500,000 for infringement of copyright (SI 2011/2222 The Patents County Court (Financial Limits) (No. 2) Order) (see Section 7.5.1.2 below).	There are a number of courts which hear criminal cases: Magistrates Court Crown Court Court of Appeal (Criminal Division) Supreme Court European Court of Justice
Who would initiate enforcement action?	In a civil case copyright infringement is treated as a private right for which it is up to the copyright holder to seek redress either through the civil courts or through other methods such as arbitration or the use of 'cease and desist' letters.	Criminal cases are deemed to be a wrong against society as a whole and are therefore prosecuted and punished by the state. Pursuing the criminals can involve the police or trading standards departments. Claimants could opt to initiate a private prosecution. In some instances organizations which represent the interests of the copyright-based industries may bring criminal prosecutions in their own right.

- using unlicensed software on the company or institution's systems with the knowledge of management
- use of the company/institution's servers to upload infringing content to the web with the knowledge of the management.

Criminal liability results when an act is performed to the extent that it affects prejudicially the owner of the copyright (see CDPA s 107(1)(e), s 107(2a)(b)). In the case of non-commercial use, a prejudicial effect on the owner could be lost sales.

In addition to the use of sections 97 and 198 of the CDPA 1988 there are also instances where organizations representing the interests of copyright-based industries have brought private prosecutions using areas of law other than copyright to bring a case, such as conspiracy to defraud. Individual claimants could potentially also choose to initiate a private prosecution.

R v Anton Benjamin Vickerman (Newcastle upon Tyne Crown Court 14 August 2012). Indictment No T2009 7188

Anton Vickerman maintained a website called Surfthechannel.com which linked to pirated copies of TV shows, movies and popular music videos, although he didn't host any infringing content on the site. He was jailed for four years after being found guilty of 'conspiracy to defraud' by facilitating the infringement of copyright, rather than being charged for copyright infringement. The Crown Prosecution Service had decided not to prosecute Mr Vickerman because of the complexity of the case and also because of the cost. The case was instead brought by the Federation Against Copyright Theft (FACT) as a private criminal prosecution. FACT filmed inside Mr Vickerman's home – with one of its agents posing as a prospective house buyer, while another FACT operative posed undercover as a potential investor in his website.

Mr Vickerman had his prison term increased by one month for committing contempt of court on the day he was sentenced.[4] The contempt of court consisted of him linking to a court document from a blog and making comments about the judge, counsel and the Federation Against Copyright Theft.

In December 2014 it was reported in Newcastle Chronicle Live[5] that Mr Vickerman was now out of prison, but that he had been back to Newcastle Crown Court for a proceeds of crime hearing. The judge ordered him to pay £73,055.79 within six months or face a further 21-month prison sentence.

7.2.8 Examples of criminal convictions for copyright infringement

- On 17 April 2013 at Harrow Crown Court a 46-year-old man was sentenced to eight weeks' imprisonment, suspended for 18 months, and ordered to carry out 150 hours of unpaid work for copying and selling copyright-infringing music CDs on eBay.

- In December 2012 David Cox – trading as Premier Videos – was convicted at Inner London Crown Court for making illegal CDs and DVDs. He was sentenced to 18 months in prison.
- In January 2013 Paul Wellings, a computer maintenance businessman from the West Midlands, was sentenced to nine months in prison by Warwickshire Crown Court for selling counterfeit music, films and games.
- Dwayne Murray, who was also known as the Reggae Doctor, was sentenced to eight months in prison on 25 February 2013 at Inner London Crown Court for making and selling counterfeit compilation albums via his website www.reggaedoctor.co.uk. Around £60,000 worth of fake records were seized at his home.
- In November 2013, Darren Clapham of Rotherham was sentenced to 14 months imprisonment at Sheffield Crown Court after he pleaded guilty to making and distributing copied music discs which he sold via a number of lists circulated to his customer base. A warrant had been served on his home in December 2012 where a vast number of masters and ready-made physical discs were seized along with computer and copying equipment.
- In December 2013, Keith Tamkin from Bognor Regis received an 18-month prison sentence after admitting offences of distributing counterfeit CDs and preloaded hard drives full of music. He also pleaded guilty to money laundering to the value of £140,000.
- In July 2013, Lester Hawkes was sentenced to 3 years and 10 months imprisonment for counterfeit DVD, CD and MP3 production, which yielded almost half a million pounds. His wife, Pauline Hawkes, also received a sentence of 21 months suspended for two years. Together they had made around £460,000 over a five-year period from selling counterfeit MP3s, DVDs and CDs.
- In October 2013, Kevin Broughton was charged with fraud and copyright offences, and given a two-year prison sentence by Sheffield Crown Court. He had created a website which illegally screened live Premiership football. He had gained over £500,000 over several years from charging subscriptions to the service.

(Source: IP crime reports of the IP crime group)

Copyright Licensing Agency v Brighton & Hove City Council (2013)

A Copyright Licensing Agency (CLA) licence is required by businesses or public sector organizations to cover a number of copying activities which are often undertaken during the course of day-to-day activities. The CLA licence allows reproduction of electronic or online publications, copying and e-mailing of press cuttings and articles or photocopying and scanning from print books.

Brighton & Hove City Council had a licence with the CLA which they cancelled in 2008. The council argued that because they had a 'no copying' policy that they did not need to renew the licence. However, evidence gathered by CLA showed that the policy had not worked and that copyright infringement was taking place. According to a CLA press release published in April 2013,[6] in an out of court settlement the council agreed to pay the CLA an undisclosed sum to cover legal costs and retrospective licence fees as well as agreeing to take a CLA licence for the future.

While the settlement involved what was originally referred to as 'an undisclosed sum', within a matter of months the *Local Government Chronicle* had published a story entitled "Copyright Agency Catches Up With Councils".[7] This fleshed out the sums involved, the information having been obtained as a result of a freedom of information (FOI) request. The response to the FOI request revealed that the council had paid over £100,000 to settle the case. This consisted of: £17,947 for an annual licence; £67,301 in backdated fees; and £16,500 contribution to the agency's legal costs, a total of £101,748.

By August 2013 the CLA were able to announce[8] that following the legal action against Brighton & Hove City Council a further 20 councils had taken out a CLA licence, and the *Local Government Chronicle* article mentioned how in the case of ten of these councils that they had also made backdated payments following advice from the agency that this would reduce the risk of legal action for retrospective copying. At the same time the CLA were still pursuing around 140 councils who did not have licences.

A BBC news online story about the case[9] tells how the CLA's legal director had disclosed that the CLA used several 'weapons' to prove copyright breaches, and that these included the use of freedom of information requests and a whistle-blowing system.

SSER Limited v The Governors of Uckfield Community College (2012) (Claim No. CC12P01789)

In October 2012 the Patents County Court held that Uckfield Community College had infringed the copyright in the works of SSER Limited, and that it had breached the terms of its licence with SSER.

SSER Limited are a provider of educational products for nursery, primary, secondary and college levels. According to *Copyright Maze*, a newsletter of Colleges Scotland, Uckfield College had been using images from SSER on its website without licence or permission.[10] The college was required within 14 days of the court order to pay SSER Limited £23,000, and this figure was inclusive of damages and costs.

Another part of the settlement was that the College was required to place on the home page of its website under the 'latest notices' column in a font size of no less than 12 a statement – the precise wording of which was given in the court order – that the college was liable for infringing the copyright of SSER Limited, which linked to the full text of the court order. The statement read: 'In a Patents County Court order dated 25th of October 2012, it was found that Uckfield Community Technology College was liable for infringing the copyright of SSER Limited following the publication of certain copyright materials on this website. A full copy of the Order may be read at www.sser.co.uk/UckfieldOrderSealed.pdf.'

Jason Sheldon v Daybrook House Promotions Limited [2013] EWPCC 26

Daybrook House Promotions Limited used an exclusive photograph taken by Jason Sheldon in order to promote its business, a dance venue in Nottingham called Rock City. The infringing photograph was of the American pop star Ke$ha and pop duo LMFAO lounging around together on a sofa with Ke$ha brandishing a bottle of champagne.

Daybrook's use of the image was unlicensed and unlawful. Sheldon originally invoiced £1351 for the infringement, that figure being based on his then understanding of the extent to which the photograph had been used. Sheldon began proceedings to recover the money he felt he was owed by using the government's money claim online procedure and this was issued in Northampton County Court. The case was subsequently transferred to the Patents County Court and a case management conference took place on 10 December 2012, by which time the photographer had found that his photograph had been published far more extensively than he originally thought and for an extended period. The court accepted that Daybrook had published the picture as part of a montage of images, in advertisements on its website, on posters of various different sizes, on flyers, and on its Rock City Facebook page. Daybrook had made no attempt to obtain permission and had disclosed none of these additional uses.

The root of the difficulty in this case was the very different view that the parties took as to what constituted a fair licence fee for the acts complained of. Judge Birss recognized that it was important to decide the question of how much the claim was worth as soon as practicable. He therefore sought to establish what would be a reasonable royalty, that is, the amount that would have been agreed between a willing licensor and a willing licensee. Daybrook contended that the value of the claim was low and should be measured in a few hundred pounds; in response to Mr Sheldon's invoice they had offered £150. To justify their assertion they relied on a quotation from the photographer David Baird where the cost was calculated using the fotoQuote software built into Mr Baird's website.

Mr Sheldon provided evidence of quotations for similar uses from Getty Images, Retna and Rex Features that ranged from £2,450 to £14,667.05.

Mr Sheldon was a professional photographer whose business was the licensing of the copyright in his photographs. For the photograph involved in this dispute he had negotiated exclusive access to the tour bus on which the picture was taken, and the picture featured award-winning and internationally renowned artists. The judge recognized that it would not be worthwhile for a photographer to go to the effort of gaining exclusive access to a location, merely to license the resulting images for a few hundred pounds. Judge Birss assessed that a fair licence fee for legitimate use would be £5,682.37 exclusive of VAT and interest. Following that hearing the two parties negotiated an overall figure covering the infringement and Sheldon's costs. Daybrook eventually agreed to pay Sheldon a sum of £20,000 following the Patents County Court decision.

7.3   Risk management

Some of the most important words and phrases in the CDPA 1988 aren't defined.

They include the terms 'fair dealing', 'substantial part', 'commercial purpose', and their definition is essential in order to work out whether or not an infringement has taken place. In the case of the phrase 'fair dealing', this would have to be determined on the basis of the facts involved in each case. The only way you would know for sure that an act of copying was indeed fair would be when the judge tells you so in court, so long as the judgment is not qualified or overturned by a superior court.

Copyright scenarios rarely have black-and-white answers which you can rely on with absolute certainty. It is therefore better to approach copyright as a question of risk management, to ask yourself what are the riskiest activities, and what you can do to minimize the risk of infringement. A useful resource is the IPR risk calculator (which was created as part of the Web2Rights OER support project): www.web2rights.com/OERIPRSupport/risk-management-calculator.

7.3.1 Levels of risk

Table 7.2 sets out the levels of risk involved in various examples of acts of copying.

Table 7.2 Levels of risk in acts of copying	
No risk	• Copying material for which you own the copyright • Copying material for any purpose for which you have obtained the rights owner's permission in writing • Copying material in accordance with any licence agreements that your organization holds • Copying material in accordance with a Creative Commons licence.
Low risk	• Single copies of short extracts of a work.
Medium risk	• Copying anything under the fair dealing exceptions[11] — research — private study — illustration for instruction — quotation — parody.
High risk	• Making and selling pirate copies of someone else's content • Illegal copies of software loaded onto your work PC • Copying commercially produced films, software and music and putting these onto your organization's network • Copying substantial portions of content belonging to a rights owner who is known to be highly litigious • Copying high-resolution versions of digital images and placing these on your company's extranet when you do not hold the rights and for which you have not obtained permission • Stealing a competitor's intellectual property.

7.3.2 Reputational risk

A good business behaves in a way that is both ethical and legal. If a civil or a criminal copyright court action takes place it is likely to generate adverse publicity; potentially it can have a significant impact on how companies and other institutions view you and it is very likely to inform their decision as to whether they wish to deal with you or do business with you. In the case of quoted companies there is the potential for reputational damage to impact negatively upon the company's share price.

7.4   Liability
7.4.1   Libraries

There have been a number of legal cases which have considered the question of whether having a photocopier in the library constitutes an incitement to infringe copyright. An important consideration in these cases has been the presence or absence of copyright warning notices, posters or supervision.

University of New South Wales v Moorhouse [1975] HCA 26 1975

This High Court of Australia case used the copying of an anthology of short stories by Frank Moorhouse as a test case to examine the meaning of the term 'authorizing' in the context of liability for authorizing infringements of copyright.

 The court held that the word 'authorizing' should be given a broad interpretation. In the Moorhouse case, the University of New South Wales had placed a number of photocopying machines in its library for the use of students. The court held that doing so without any copyright warning notices or supervision constituted an invitation for the students to infringe copyright and that such an invitation amounted to authorization of any infringements of copyright that had been committed or were likely to be committed as a consequence of that invitation.

 In response to the Moorhouse decision, section 39A of the (Australian) Copyright Act 1968 was introduced. Entitled 'Infringing copies made on machines installed in libraries and archives', it provides protection with regard to photocopiers installed in libraries or archives so long as a copyright notice is prominently displayed.

CCH Canadian Ltd v Law Society of Upper Canada [2004] 1 SCR 339

In March 2004 the Supreme Court of Canada unanimously ruled that the Law Society of Upper Canada's dealings with the works of three legal publishers through its custom photocopy service were 'research based and fair'. The key question considered in this case was whether the Law Society breached copyright by either:

- providing a photocopy request service in which single copies of publishers' works were reproduced and sent to library users, or
- maintaining self-service photocopiers for the use of library users.

The Supreme Court of Canada held that the Court of Appeal had erred in finding that LSUC's posting of a notice next to self-service photocopiers – warning that it would not be responsible for any copies made in infringement of copyright – constituted an express acknowledgement that copiers would be used in an illegal manner. The court held that libraries and their users were not in a master–servant or employer–employee relationship such that the library can be said to exercise control over its users who might commit infringement and that it could therefore be presumed that they were not authorizing patrons to breach copyright laws.

The key lesson from this case is that librarians should post appropriately worded signs, notices, or posters next to all self-service photocopying machines. These should be placed in a prominent position and should warn library users of the implications of breaching copyright law, and what actions on their part may constitute a breach. Where signs, posters or notices are used in conjunction with a written copyright policy which is enforced, the risk of the library being held liable for authorizing infringement by placing self-service copiers in the library is reduced.

7.4.2   Library users

Librarians working in not-for-profit publicly accessible libraries can supply their users with a single copy of a journal article or a reasonable proportion of any other published work where this is in response to a request from a library user. Where the copy is made under the library exception in CDPA 1988 section 42A, the library user is required to provide the librarian with a declaration in writing. Library users are required to confirm:

- that they haven't previously been supplied with a copy of the material by any library
- that they require the copy for non-commercial research or private study
- that they will only use it for those purposes, and that they will not supply the copy to any other person, and
- that to the best of their knowledge no one with whom they work or study has made or intends to make at or about the same time a request for substantially the same material for substantially the same purpose.

Where a library user completes a declaration form and this includes a false statement, it is the library user who would be liable for the infringement of copyright as if they had made the copy themselves. The librarian is, in effect, given protection from liability for copyright infringement as long as the conditions laid out in the legislation have been met. If a legal case were brought against the librarian, the written declaration completed by the library user would need to be produced as evidence. Publicly accessible libraries need to keep the written declarations for a period of six years plus the current year. Since June 2014 it has been possible for library users to provide the written declaration electronically.

7.4.3   Directors

A director of a 'body corporate' can potentially be held to be personally liable for copyright infringement under section 110 of the CDPA 1988. The term 'body corporate' means a legal entity such as a company, an institution or an association. The wording of section 110 says:

110 Offence by body corporate: liability of officers

(1)   Where an offence under section 107 committed by a body corporate is proved to have been committed with the consent or connivance of a director, manager, secretary or other similar officer of the body, or a person purporting to act in any such capacity, he as well as the body corporate is guilty of the offence and liable to be proceeded against and punished accordingly.

(2)   In relation to a body corporate whose affairs are managed by its members "director" means a member of the body corporate.

Source: The National Archives, 2015

IT Human Resources PLC v David Land [2014] EWHC 3812.

In this case Mr Land was an IT consultant and computer programmer. He had worked for and been a director of the recruitment company IT Human Resources PLC. During his time with the company he had created a software system to help the company with its work in the recruitment of IT technical staff. Mr Land was found to have infringed the company's copyright in the software system by providing it to a competitor without the company's consent. He was also held to have breached his fiduciary duties as a director pursuant to s 1157 of the Companies Act 2006.

An interesting point about the case relates to the timing of the legal action. Even though the infringement occurred over six years before the action was brought, the company was not barred by statute from bringing the legal action because its knowledge of the infringing activity had been delayed by the director's deliberate concealment. The limitation period was therefore extended pursuant to section 32 of the Limitation Act 1980 on the grounds of that deliberate concealment.

Naxos Rights International Ltd v Project Management (Borders) Ltd & Salmon [2012] CSOH 158.

In this Scottish case, the Outer House of the Court of Session in Scotland deemed a company director to be guilty in his own right of copyright infringement as well as the company of which he was a director: www.scotscourts.gov.uk/opinions/2012CSOH158.html.

Naxos Rights International Ltd trades as a record label which commissions recordings or obtains the rights to exploit works of classical music which it sells both on CD and by digital download from its website www.classicsonline.com and from third-party websites such as iTunes and Amazon. Naxos sought damages for copyright infringement on the grounds that Project Management (Borders) Ltd had infringed its copyright by offering for sale and licence copies of recordings in which Naxos owned the rights – the recordings in question being of Vivaldi's *Four Seasons* and the song *Joy to the World*. Naxos alleged that the infringing acts done by the limited company were authorized or procured by its director, Mr Salmon, who was the company's sole director and shareholder, and that he was therefore joint and severally liable for any damage.

Mr Salmon relied on the principle in Saloman v Saloman and Co. Ltd [1897] AC 22 that the acts weren't his, but were those of the company, for which he wasn't liable. But the court noted that 'the fact that he was a director of the company does not place him in some protected category'. Citing the words of Lord Templeman in CBS Songs v Amstrad Consumer Electronics PLC [1988] AC 1013, liability of a joint tortfeasor may arise where the individual 'intends and procures and shares a common design that the infringement takes place'. The test was whether (a) he procured the breaches of copyright by the company and (b) he and the company, both separate legal entities, were acting in concert with one another pursuant to a common design in the infringement.

The court was in no doubt that Salmon was personally liable for the infringements of copyright. The domain name of the website www.royalty-free-classical-music.org was registered in the name of Mr Salmon as an individual, but Mr Salmon claimed that the site was 'operated' by the limited company. The judge was satisfied that the website was in fact operated together by the limited company and by Mr Salmon. At paragraph 64 the judgment says 'The true position is, in my view, that Mr Salmon was acting not only as a director of the company but also as an individual setting up the website and putting or causing to be put infringing material on it for sale. This makes him liable as a principal, not only for his own acts but also for those of the company on the basis both of procurement and of acting in concert with the company for a common purpose.'

7.4.4   Intermediary service providers

Article 12 of the E-commerce Directive on 'Mere conduits' ensures that information society service providers are not liable for the information transmitted across their networks in cases where they do not initiate the transmission, they don't select the receiver of the transmission, and they do not select or modify the information contained in the transmission. Where an intermediary service provider becomes aware that copyright infringement is occurring, it needs to act promptly by taking down the infringing content, because reliance on the innocent disseminator defence requires that it does not have actual knowledge of the infringing activity.

7.4.4.1   Free and open Wi-Fi networks

If a person offers access to the internet without the need for a password to be entered can they be considered to be a 'mere conduit' under the E-Commerce Directive 2000/31/EC in circumstances where an unknown user sends a piece of copyright-infringing music across that internet connection? This is the subject of a European Court of Justice case (Case C-484/14 McFadden) where a regional court in Munich referred a number of questions to the CJEU in order to clarify the liability for third-party copyright infringements of commercial providers of free and open Wi-Fi access. Once the case has been decided it should give clarity and legal certainty to the liability of wireless operators.

The background to the case is as follows. An entrepreneur, Tobias McFadden, operates a wireless local area network (WLAN) in his store which isn't secured by a password and which can be used free of charge by business partners and visitors. A record label notified Mr McFadden that it had identified that his network had been used for illegal file-sharing in breach of its copyright. The 'mere conduit' defence is available to internet service providers as information society services. So a crucial question will be whether Mr McFadden can be considered to be an ISP. One stumbling block to overcome will be the way in which recital 17 of the directive uses a definition of information society services which 'covers any service normally provided for remuneration'.

7.4.5   Employees

Employees can be held to be personally liable for copyright infringement in some circumstances.

Phonographic Performance Ltd v John Nash (T/A Charlie Wrights International) (2014) EWHC Chancery Division, 23 October 2014.

Phonographic Performance Ltd (PPL) sued Nash, the premises licence holder and designated premises supervisor of a music bar and nightclub, for copyright infringement and sought summary judgment on the basis that Nash had either played musical recordings at the venue without being licensed or permitted to do so, or had authorized others to do so, or both. PPL asserted that Nash was well aware that PPL held the public performance rights in the recordings and they therefore pursued an injunction to prevent Nash from repeatedly infringing its copyright. They sought the injunction because they believed that Nash wouldn't stop infringing the copyrights of its members unless he was restrained from doing so.

Nash argued that the venue was operated by a company that employed him as a manager, that he had never traded from the venue on his own account and resisted the application for summary judgment. He claimed not to be the 'controlling mind' of any company operating from that address. He also applied for two previous orders to be set aside on the ground that they violated his right to a fair trial since they were made in his absence. Judge Pelling QC took the view that being an employee was not a defence to copyright infringement and that Nash could not avoid personal liability on that basis.

7.4.6 Employers

It is worth bearing in mind that an employer can be vicariously liable for the actions of its employees. Vicarious liability is where someone is held to be responsible for actions or omissions of another person. In the context of the workplace an employer can he held liable for the acts or omissions of its employees, and the actions committed by employees for which the employer can be held responsible include breaches of copyright. The key question in a vicarious liability case would be whether the employee was acting in a personal capacity or whether they were doing so in the course of their employment.

There are practical steps which an employer can take in order to reduce the risk of being held to be vicariously liable for breaches of copyright undertaken by its employees:

- One example would be to have a formal policy on intellectual property rights in the staff handbook. The company should from time to time draw this to the attention of staff where appropriate. If the copyright policy is updated, that would be an opportune time to remind employees of the policy. It should also be drawn to the attention of new joiners. If the organization found infringing copies of music or films downloaded from file-sharing sites on its servers, that would also be a good time to remind staff members of their obligations.
- Another example would be the provision of regular training and awareness sessions covering copyright law, with guidance as to what is and what is not acceptable.
- Another would be to provide staff with a central point for copyright queries if they are unsure as to what is allowed, and to ensure that this is well publicized.

7.5 Dispute resolution

★ There are a number of ways in which a dispute could potentially be resolved. A useful resource is Resolving IP Disputes, IP Health Check 5, rev. edn, IPO, November 2013, https://www.gov.uk/government/collections/ip-for-business-events-guidance-tools-and-case-studies.

7.5.1 Disputes with publishers or with aggregators

The route chosen to resolve a dispute may well depend on the client's main objective. If the main objective is to minimize cost, then non-binding mediation would be the best option. If the main objective is to get a speedy decision, then non-binding mediation would again be the best route. But if the main objective is to set a legal precedent, or to get vindication, the best option would be to go to court. If the main objective is to obtain a neutral opinion, this could be achieved either through arbitration or by going to court.

7.5.1.1 High Court

A court case would be extremely costly, which is why there are relatively few cases decided in court. For example, the report *An Economic Analysis of Copyright, Secondary Copyright and Collective Licensing* (PwC, 2011) said that there had been 67 fair dealing decisions in the courts since 1978, or an average of two cases per year. These figures were attributed by PwC to data gathered by the British Copyright Council and used in the BCC's submission to the *Hargreaves Review*.

Wherever possible going to the High Court to settle a copyright infringement case should be avoided, and only contemplated as a last resort. It would almost always be better to see if the matter could be resolved by other means. If the matter cannot be resolved informally it may be necessary to initiate legal proceedings. But this would only be advisable for a copyright owner if:

- they can prove that they own the rights in the work
- they can prove that there has been an infringement of their rights
- the value of a successful legal action outweighs the costs of bringing the proceedings.

If you are the owner of the rights which have been infringed, you should consider the use of the notice and takedown procedure, arbitration or mediation as a way of resolving a dispute.

If you are the one being accused of copyright infringement, one thing that you should do is to ensure that the disputed activity does not continue. This might, for example, require you to promptly take down the disputed content from your website or to put a stop to a copying activity which has been occurring on a regular basis with the disputed material.

7.5.1.2 Intellectual Property Enterprise Court

Intellectual property cases are heard in the Chancery Division of the High Court or by the Intellectual Property Enterprise Court (IPEC, which was formerly known as the Patents County Court. IPEC cases are allocated either to the multi-track or the small-claims track:

- The IPEC small-claims track is a forum where the most straightforward of intellectual property claims with a low financial value can be heard and decided. It is only suitable for claims where the amount in dispute (excluding costs) is £10,000 or less.
- The IPEC multi-track is suitable for claims over £10,000 but not exceeding £500,000.

★ A guide to the small-claims track, *Guide to the Intellectual Property Enterprise Court Small Claims Track* is available at www.justice.gov.uk/downloads/courts/patents-court/patents-court-small-claims.pdf and sets out the procedure involved in the small-claims track.

7.5.1.3   Alternative dispute resolution

Alternative dispute resolution or (ADR) is a term used to describe a number of different ways in which a dispute might be settled. These could include the use of arbitration or mediation.

Mediation is certainly a cheaper and quicker means of resolving a dispute than litigation and the outcome is usually beneficial to all parties. A court would expect you to have made efforts to resolve your dispute before initiating legal proceedings and the use of mediation would be one option that could be used for that purpose. Mediation has the potential to result in a strong ongoing business relationship through licensing or commercial agreements, because it could involve discussing a wider range of topics than the issues that are the subject of the dispute.

The Intellectual Property Office provides a mediation service to resolve intellectual property disputes. There is a charge for the use of this service. They have accredited mediators who can help you resolve copyright disputes, although the service can also be used to resolve disputes involving other intellectual property rights.

Arbitration is a procedure in which the parties agree to submit their dispute to an arbitrator who can make a binding decision on the dispute. By choosing arbitration the parties are opting for a private dispute resolution procedure instead of going to court. Arbitration can only take place if both parties agree to it. Together they select an arbitrator with the requisite industry specialist expertise, and the ability to choose an arbitrator is one of the main advantages of arbitration. The procedure is confidential, as is the award. Arbitration can be suitable where it is urgent that the matter be settled, because court procedures could take longer and be more drawn-out.

7.5.2   Notice and takedown procedure

A notice and takedown procedure can be used as a way of dealing with instances where content has inadvertently been used without the knowledge or consent of the rights owner. It provides an easy way for the rights holder to get in touch with the infringer in order to alert them to the fact that they are aware of their infringing use of the content, and request that it be promptly removed or taken down.

If a website has a formal notice and takedown procedure in place, this will lay out how the procedure works. If someone is concerned that they have found material on a website for which that site doesn't have the necessary permission they should look to see if the site has a notice and takedown policy. The policy will set out what information you need to include when making a complaint, and who to contact.

7.5.3 Disputes with collective management organizations

In recent years there have been a number of new provisions relating to the regulation of the collective management organizations (CMOs). These include:

- The Enterprise and Regulatory Reform Act 2013 section 77 and schedule 22 on the licensing of copyright and performers rights
- The Copyright (Regulation of Relevant Licensing Bodies) Regulations 2014: SI 2014/898.

In addition, Directive 2014/26/EU on collective management of copyright and related rights and multi-licensing of rights in musical works for online use in the internal market is due for implementation in UK law by 10 April 2016.

7.5.3.1 *CMO codes of practice*

Licensing bodies were encouraged by the government to introduce self-regulatory codes of practice, and the main collective management organizations do now have codes of practice in place. Since the coming into force of SI 2014/898 on the regulation of the licensing bodies there is now a statutory minimum set of standards, which means that the CMOs' codes of practice are required to meet those minimum standards with regard to transparency and behaviour, and it also requires that they have formal complaints procedures in place. The government has backstop legislative powers to direct licensing bodies to adopt a code of practice which can be used either where a licensing body doesn't have a code of practice, or where its code doesn't comply with the minimum standards set out in the schedule to SI 2014/898.

A licensing code reviewer appointed by the Secretary of State reviews the codes of practice of the licensing bodies and reports on how their codes relate to the minimum standards and also on their compliance with the code (see Independent Code Review, www.independentcodereview.org.uk). The Secretary of State can impose financial penalties of up to £50,000 where the licensing bodies have failed to comply with their obligations.

If a licensing body is aggrieved at the imposition of a code of practice or the amount of a financial penalty imposed upon them they can appeal to the First-tier Tribunal. The First-tier Tribunal consists of seven chambers. Copyright licensing falls under The General Regulatory Chamber. It hears appeals against decisions of the Secretary of State for Business Innovation and Skills and the Comptroller

General of Patents Designs and Trade Marks under The Copyright (Regulation of Relevant Licensing Bodies) Regulations 2014 and The Copyright and Rights in Performances (Licensing of Orphan Works) Regulations 2014: SI 2014/2863.

Regulation 7 of The Copyright (Regulation of Relevant Licensing Bodies) Regulations 2014: SI 2014/898 enables the Secretary of State to appoint an ombudsman. Relevant licensing bodies, licensees or someone on whose behalf a relevant licensing body is authorized to negotiate may refer a dispute about a licensing body's compliance with its code of practice or other matter to the licensing code ombudsman. The Ombudsman Services (www.ombudsman-services.org) provides dispute resolution for the copyright licensing industry. It covers complaints from licensees relating to the licences offered by the CLA, ERA, NLA, PRS and PPL. It also deals with complaints from members of collective management organizations including ALCS, BECS (which enforces the rights of members of Equity, the trade union for professional performers and creative practitioners), DACS, Directors UK (which represents film and television directors) and PLS.

7.5.3.2   Copyright Tribunal

The primary purpose of the Copyright Tribunal is to resolve commercial licensing disputes between the collecting societies and the licensees who use copyright material within their organization. The role of the Tribunal is to determine the reasonableness of the commercial terms of the licence. Its decisions are legally binding and can only be appealed on a point of law. Notable cases relevant to information professionals which were heard before the Copyright Tribunal are:

- Universities UK v Copyright Licensing Agency Limited and Design and Artists Copyright Society Limited. Case nos: CT 71/00, 72/00, 73/00, 74/00, 75/01
- Meltwater Holding BV v Newspaper Licensing Agency Limited CT114/09 (this case was also brought before the High Court and subsequently went to the Court of Appeal, the Supreme Court and the European Court of Justice to determine whether or not the NLA had a right to require media monitoring organizations to take out a licence with the NLA in order to be able to send their clients links to stories on free to access newspaper publisher websites, and also require the clients of those media monitoring organizations to take out a licence in order to be able to click on the hyperlinks to those stories). See p. 81 for more details.

7.6   Compliance with licence terms

Another aspect of copyright compliance is where an institution has entered into a licence agreement. This could be directly with a publisher, it could be with an aggregator or it could be with a collective management organization.

It is important to ensure that the licensee complies with the licence terms. If we were to take as an example a business licence with the Copyright Licensing Agency, this would mean:

- keeping within the extent limits (one article from a journal, one chapter from a book or 5% of extracts, or in the case of a published report of judicial proceedings, the entire report of a single case)
- ensuring that you don't store licensed copies on your organization's intranet for more than 30 days
- where licensed copies are supplied to any UK regulatory authority, ensuring that they are accompanied by a copyright notice using the words of, or substantially similar to, those set out in the business licence terms and conditions: 'This document has been supplied under a CLA licence. It is protected by copyright . . .'
- not copying any excluded material (that means not copying anything in the list of excluded categories or excluded works).

If a proposed licence doesn't seem to work for you, it is important to make that known to the licensor before entering into an agreement. You should do everything you can to negotiate an agreement which better addresses your requirements. Don't just sign up to the agreement and then ignore the terms you didn't like (see also Section 4.4 on p. 89 on negotiating licence agreements).

7.7   Copyright policies

There are a number of objectives that can be achieved by having a copyright policy in place:

- It will help you reduce organizational risk of infringing third-party copyrights by raising awareness of copyright amongst employees, and what is expected of them.
- It will help you protect your organization's own intellectual property.
- If your organization is accused of copyright infringement it will help to demonstrate that you are taking copyright compliance seriously.

A copyright policy should aim to answer the sorts of questions that are commonly asked. It should provide clear instruction on what is and what is not allowed, and as such it ought to be thought of as an essential tool to help reduce the risks of liability for copyright infringement. EIFL (which stands for Electronic Information for Libraries) has a useful guide to developing a library copyright

✱ policy. The guide is intended to highlight issues when considering the creation of a copyright policy for your library, how to go about drafting the policy, and the sorts of elements that it might contain.[12]

In developing a copyright policy, there are a number of things to consider: the audience that the policy is aimed at – it may be worth developing a very brief statement for library users, and a more detailed one for library staff; and what would be the most suitable format. For example: for library users the best format might be a one-page sheet arranged as a poster which contains the key messages that you want to convey; given that there is a limit on what you can cover in a single page, you might want to supplement this with a set of frequently asked questions which is based on the types of copying activity which are most often undertaken within the organization, and the questions that are commonly asked. At the time of compiling the FAQs you could ask people to suggest topics that should be covered. The FAQs could be made available on your intranet. The FAQs can be considered to be a dynamic document which you add to and update as required, and you could include a facility on the intranet for staff to be able to suggest other questions to add.

What should the policy cover? It could include topics such as the ones listed below:

- What can I copy?
- How long does copyright last?
- What is fair dealing (for research, private study, quotation, illustration for instruction, etc.)?
- The copyright exceptions most relevant to your organization.
- Guidance on copying activities (if there are particular types of copying activity that are regularly undertaken, the policy should give some guidance on these copying activities – for example, if your users regularly copy digital images which they found on the internet, or if maps are frequently copied, or if your users regularly use government and parliamentary material.)
- A summary of the key points of any licences you hold, and what these do and don't cover (such as licences from the Copyright Licensing Agency, NLA Media Access, etc.

As part of the process of drafting a copyright policy you might also want to look at examples from other organizations to see if there is anything you might have missed or which it would be useful to add.

The copyright policy should be written in plain English. If the policy is riddled with legal jargon it could be unintelligible to your intended audience. If it isn't written in a way that is clear and intelligible it could put people off reading through it. It should also give details of who to contact for advice on copyright matters. Copyright is a complex topic, and no copyright policy can possibly cover all the questions people might have. It is important that everyone knows who to contact if they have a copyright query, especially if someone has a complex copyright problem.

Once you have prepared a draft of the policy, it would be worth asking your in-house lawyer or legal team if they could read through it in case there is anything that needs to be amended. When the copyright policy wording has been finalized, the next thing is raising awareness of the policy. The copyright policy should be actively promoted through an education and awareness programme for library staff and users. If there is a well established process of new staff inductions, the copyright policy could be covered as part of this.

Two useful resources in creating a copyright policy are: ★

Copyright Clearance Center (2011) *10 Tips for Creating a Copyright Policy: practical steps to help you comply with copyright law.*

EIFL (2012) *Developing a Library Copyright Policy: an EIFL guide.*

7.8 Copyright training, education and awareness
7.8.1 Training

There are a number of regular training courses held by organizations such as:

- TFPL, www.tfpl.com
- Aslib, www.aslib.com/training
- LIS-Copyseek, www.jiscmail.ac.uk/lis-copyseek, organize occasional training events
- CILIP's UK eInformation Group, www.ukeig.org.uk/training
- ALPSP eLearning, http://elearning.alpsp.org, offers a course on international copyright.

On-site courses tailored to the needs of the client institution are also available through:

- CILIP, www.cilip.org.uk/cilip/products-and-services/onsite-training
- TFPL, www.tfpl.com.

Postgraduate qualifications in copyright and intellectual property law are available from the following two institutions:

- King's College London offers a postgraduate diploma/Master's degree in UK, US and EU copyright law. For further information go to www.kcl.ac.uk/law/research/centres/european/programmes/copyright.aspx.
- Queen Mary University of London offers a Master of Laws in intellectual

property law either part time or full time. For further information go to www.law.qmul.ac.uk/postgraduate/courses/items/138028.html.

7.8.2   Education and awareness

If there is a person within your institution who is in charge of dealing with copyright issues, they may provide in-house training on a regular basis, or on request.

In late 2014 Dr Jane Secker and Chris Morrison undertook research into the levels of copyright literacy amongst professionals in UK information, cultural and heritage institutions. This research[13] forms part of an international project originating in the National Library of Bulgaria. The survey findings give us a clearer picture about the level of copyright knowledge of information professionals, and where there are gaps. International copyright law and international copyright organizations were two areas where there was the least knowledge; and over half of the respondents to the survey weren't familiar or were only slightly familiar with clearing rights. Another notable finding from the survey was that over 90% of respondents believe that it is necessary for intellectual property/copyright issues to be included in the continuing education of LIS and cultural heritage professionals.

In a US study[14] the evidence revealed that while library deans and directors had a basic knowledge of copyright law concepts, it was unclear as to whether their understanding was sufficient to provide a sound basis for developing and sustaining operational policies and strategic directions for their libraries.

Mike Weatherley, who stood down at the 2015 general election, was the MP for Hove and Portslade and the Prime Minister's Intellectual Property Advisor between 2013 and 2014. In that capacity he wrote a report, *Copyright Education and Awareness: a discussion paper*, which stresses the need to raise awareness of copyright and intellectual property issues. In the report he says that 'Education and consumer awareness programmes that seek to change behaviour or influence future actions are essential for nurturing a greater culture of respect and value for the UK's creative economy and to negate the impact of infringement'. Chapter 3 of the report is entitled 'The copyright education and awareness landscape', but it doesn't acknowledge the important role that LIS professionals can and do play in raising awareness of the need to respect copyright law.

The Intellectual Property Awareness Network (www.ipaware.net) is a network of professional and business organizations with a shared interest in improving general awareness and understanding of intellectual property rights.

★   The Copyright User portal designed by CREATe (http://copyrightuser.org) is an independent online resource which aims to make UK copyright law accessible to creators, media professionals, entrepreneurs, students and members of the public.

The Copyright Hub website (www.copyrighthub.co.uk) can help people who ★ need to get permission to use someone else's work, or who want to know how copyright relates to their own work.

The Intellectual Property Office provide a number of tools and resources to help raise awareness and understanding of intellectual property issues. These include:

- IP for business tools (IPO)
  https://www.gov.uk/government/publications/intellectual-property-for-business. These include:
  — IP Equip, an e-learning tool to help businesses and their advisors understand intellectual property rights (also available as an app)
  — IP Health Check, an online tool to help answer questions about how to protect and exploit intellectual property assets such as artistic designs, technology or the brand of a product or process
  — IP Master Class, a specialist course to enable people to develop a detailed understanding of IP and its relationship with business, culture and the economy.
- IP tutor (www.ipo.gov.uk/blogs/iptutor), an online learning tool aimed at universities to help students understand how IP impacts upon them, both at the university and beyond.

7.9   Ethical and professional issues and conflicts

Copyright compliance is not merely a legal issue, it is also an ethical one. CILIP's Ethical Principles for Library and Information Professionals state that the conduct of members should be characterized by a number of general principles and values, and that one of these involves 'Respect for, and understanding of, the integrity of information items and for the intellectual effort of those who created them'. CILIP's Code of Professional Practice (2012 version) sets out a number of points with regard to professional behaviour. In the section on responsibilities to information and its users, the Code states that members of CILIP should 'defend the legitimate needs and interests of information users, while upholding the moral and legal rights of the creators and distributors of intellectual property'. In the section on responsibilities to colleagues and the information community members are also required to refrain from any behaviour in the course of their work which might bring the information profession into disrepute.

A key role of information professionals is to provide information to their users. But in fulfilling this function they can regularly find themselves being asked to provide copyright-protected content to library users whilst on the other hand knowing that copyright owners want to be paid for the use of their works.

If you work for a commercial organization, don't ask colleagues you know who work for other organizations to provide you with an article from a journal to which you don't subscribe. If you need the article:

- Check to see if it has been made available through open access. It could be that a version of the article is freely accessible on the web through an institutional repository. Portal sites such as ROAR (http://roar.eprints.org/content.html) and OpenDOAR (www.opendoar.org/search.php) can be used to search across the contents of many institutional repositories through a single search.
- Where necessary contact the vendor and ask if you can purchase a one-off copy.

There may well be situations where you might be able – from a technical, though not from a legal point of view – to access content that your company doesn't subscribe to. In such instances it is important to be guided by one's ethical principles (and for CILIP members these are set out in its ethical principles for library and information professionals). Below are a couple of scenarios where one's ethical values could be put to the test:

- The 'Access to Research' initiative of the Publishers Licensing Society makes available a wide range of journals through participating public libraries. However, one of the terms and conditions of use is that 'I will only use the publications . . . for my own personal, e.g. non-commercial research and private study' (see http://accesstoresearch.pls.org.uk).
- You can access a database or an e-journal through your membership of the local public library, or you are studying part-time and can access a publication through the university's electronic resources. Remember that the licences will have restrictions on usage. Access to a university's electronic resources would almost certainly be licensed on terms which expressly forbade their use for commercial purposes.

7.10   Copyright clearance process

In 2000 Elizabeth Gadd wrote a detailed report[15] on copyright clearance, for which she undertook a survey of staff responsible for clearance within higher education institutions. A number of respondents to the survey expressed concern over the lack of awareness by their internal customers as to how complex the copyright clearance process is. Gadd identified a number of problems, and these included insufficient bibliographic information being provided as well as unrealistic time-scales. Gadd found that while two weeks was the median length of time taken to get permission, the mean was a month, and that it was certainly not uncommon for the process to take two to three months. Especially in the corporate sector, telling someone to 'hang on a month while I sort out the necessary permissions' would hardly go down well.

Steps involved in the copyright clearance process include:

- establishing whether permission is needed
- identifying the rights that you need permission for
- identifying the rights owner
- contacting the rights owner
- negotiating whether a payment is required, and if so, for how much
- getting the permission in writing
- when using the work, giving proper acknowledgement (the precise form in which acknowledgement should be given may be specified in the licence agreement).

It may also be necessary to chase up the rights holder to get a response. One thing to bear in mind is that there is nothing in the law which requires a rights holder to respond to a permission request; but a lack of response should not be taken as justification for going ahead with the copying. By contacting the rights holder you will have alerted them that you want to copy their content, and it could be that the reason they didn't answer your request is because they are waiting to see if you go ahead with the use of their work without hearing back from them so that they can demand a substantial sum for the infringing use of their content. The National Council of Archives' response to the *Gowers Review of Intellectual Property* cites an example of a local historian who was faced with a demand for £20,000 immediately after his book was published for using a photograph without permission where he had spent considerable effort in his search for the copyright owner, and where the book was printed with the usual calls for the owner to come forward.

7.10.1   Tracing rights owners

Copyright is automatic, without the need to go through a formal registration process. As a result there isn't a comprehensive database of copyright works and their rights holders. Indeed, it would breach the Berne Convention to force the creators of new works to go through a registration process before their works qualify for protection. Article 5(2) of the Convention says that the enjoyment and the exercise of the rights (which are detailed within the Convention wording) shall not be subject to any formality. Even if there were a single database, it would only be reliable if it was constantly updated with any changes of copyright ownership. Copyright is, after all, a property right and as such can be bought, sold or given away. There are, nevertheless, a number of databases which can help to identify copyright holders, and these are shown in Figure 7.3 on the next page. A useful resource is: JISC (2009) *IPR Toolkit: overview, key issues and toolkit elements*, produced for the SCA IPR Consultancy by Naomi Korn, http://webarchive.nationalarchives. gov.uk/20140702233839/http://www.jisc.ac.uk/media/documents/publications/ scaiprtoolkitoverview.pdf (see *Getting permissions* within section 4 of the toolkit).

The Content Map (www.thecontentmap.com) is a portal which brings together film, TV, music, publishing, video games and sports broadcasters to provide a single site to demonstrate the wealth of legal services available to UK consumers. The Police IP Crime Unit directs visitors to seized domains to The Content Map.

Find Any Film (www.findanyfilm.com) is a database of films that are legally available across all formats.

The Copyright Hub (www.copyrighthub.co.uk) is a site which aims to help if people want to get permission to use someone else's work.

WATCH (Writers Artists and their Copyright Holders): http://norman.hrc.utexas.edu/watch.

VIAF (Virtual International Authority Files): http://viaf.org.

FOB (Firms Out of Business): http://norman.hrc.utexas.edu/watch/fob.cfm.

ARROW (Accessible Registries of Rights Information and Orphan Works): www.arrow-net.eu.

Orphan works database (OHIM): https://oami.europa.eu/ohimportal/en/web/observatory/orphan-works-database.

Orphan works register (IPO): www.orphanworkslicensing.service.gov.uk/view-register.

In the case of orphan works there are lists of sources which must be searched as part of a diligent search for the owner of the rights. Schedule ZA1 – 'Certain permitted uses of orphan works' is inserted into the CDPA 1988 by The Copyright and Rights in Performances (Certain Permitted Uses of Orphan Works) Regulations 2014: SI 2014/2861. Part 2 of the Schedule contains a list of sources to be searched during a diligent search.

Figure 7.3 *Databases for identifying copyright holders*

Notes

1   A consultation on changes to the penalties for copyright offences was launched in July 2015:
    https://www.gov.uk/government/uploads/system/uploads/attachment_data/file/446515/Changes_to_penalties_for_online_copyright_infringement.pdf.

2   In Scotland, if the claim is complex or valuable, the Court of Session can be used. There are no limits to the legal costs or damages that can be claimed.

3   Speculative invoicing and 'pay up or else' schemes for copyright infringement, https://www.citizensadvice.org.uk/consumer/phones-tv-internet-and-computers/the-internet-filesharing-and-copyright/speculative-invoicing-and-pay-up-or-else-schemes-for-copyright-infringement/.

4   Surfthechannel Owner Jailed for Contempt of Court, *BBC News Online*, 21 November 2012, www.bbc.co.uk/news/uk-england-tyne-20435505.

5   Gateshead Movie Pirate Who Made £1.25m Must Pay Back £73,000, 17 December 2014, www.chroniclelive.co.uk/news/north-east-news/gateshead-movie-pirate-who-made-8302799.

6   *CLA Legal Action Forces Brighton & Hove City Council to Take a Licence,* CLA

press release, 11 April 2013.

7   Keeling, R. (2013) Copyright Agency Catches up with Councils, *Local Government Chronicle*, 21 August.

8   *Twenty New Councils Take Copyright Licence Following CLA Legal Action*, CLA press release, 19 August 2013.

9   Brighton and Hove City Council Pays for Copyright Breaches, *BBC News Online*, 11 April 2013.

10 Uckfield Community College Penalised for Infringement, *Copyright Maze*, 11, February 2013.

11 The reason that 'fair dealing' copies appear under Medium Risk is because what would constitute a fair and reasonable copy of an extract from a work cannot be judged solely in quantitative terms. It is also a qualitative issue. The only way you would know for sure that the copying was indeed fair would be when a judge told you in court that this was the case; and even then it would be dependent upon whether the ruling was overturned by a higher court.

12 EIFL (2012) *Developing a Copyright Policy: an EIFL guide*, www.eifl.net.

13 The results were published as *UK Copyright Literary Survey: summary report* by Chris Morrison and Jane Seeker, June 2015.   ★

14 Eye, John (2013) Knowledge Level of Library Deans and Directors in Copyright Law, *Journal of Librarianship and Scholarly Communication*, http://dx.doi.org/10.7710/2162-3309.1103.

15 Gadd, Elizabeth (2000) *Clearing the Way: copyright clearance in UK libraries*, Loughborough University.

CHAPTER 8

Copyright for the corporate sector

This chapter looks at copyright issues from the perspective of the corporate sector. It considers those changes to the copyright exceptions (Section 8.1) which are of benefit to the corporate sector, and explores the reasons why many of the copyright exceptions cannot be used by corporate library and information professionals. Given the limited use that corporate librarians can make of the copyright exceptions, the chapter looks at how licensing (Section 8.2) can be used as a way of making copies of content legitimately even where this is for a commercial purpose. The chapter ends with a brief look at how to search for images where the use is commercial (Section 8.3); and also gives details of a copyright clearance service for obtaining permission to copy works (Section 8.4).

8.1   The copyright exceptions

Information professionals working in the corporate sector will find that their ability to copy works under the exceptions is far more limited than would be the case in other sectors such as the public library sector or the educational sector. Why might this be so? And what options are open to them?

8.1.1   Purpose for which the copying is done

One fundamental issue relates to the purpose for which the copying is done. A number of the exceptions only cover copying where the purpose is non-commercial. That is true, for example, of the following exceptions:

- research and private study (section 29 of CDPA 1988)
- illustration for instruction (section 32)
- text and data analysis (section 29A)
- personal copies for private use (section 28B).

To avoid any doubt, I should make clear that whether the copying is being done for commercial or non-commercial purposes is not dependent upon the nature of the organization doing the copying. It is all down to the purpose for which the copy is made, and as a result that can impact across all types of organization, whether they are commercial or not-for-profit. However, the number of instances where a company can be said to be doing things for a non-commercial purpose will be extremely limited. Examples might include:

- pro-bono work undertaken by a firm of solicitors, provided that it wasn't done in the hope of generating subsequent fee-paying work
- work done by a student who is being sponsored by a company for their degree
- articles copied for CPD activity, where the CPD activity isn't paid for by the company and where it isn't directed at improving earning potential.

Significant changes were made to the copyright exceptions during the course of 2014. These included the introduction of a series of entirely new exceptions:

- personal copies for private use (Section 28B)
- text and data mining (Section 29A)
- making works available through dedicated terminals (Section 40B)
- certain permitted uses of orphan works (Section 44B)
- quotation (Section 30 (1ZA))
- caricature, parody or pastiche (Section 30A).

However, only two of these new exceptions permit copying where it is for a commercial purpose. They are the quotation exception and the exception for caricature, parody or pastiche. The revised impact assessment which was issued when SI 2014/2356 (www.legislation.gov.uk/uksi/2014/2356/contents/made) was published anticipates that the average 'fair' quotation would be of the order of 50 words (www.legislation.gov.uk/ukia/2014/275/pdfs/ukia_20140275_en.pdf). Of the exceptions which were already in place prior to the 2014 changes, there are a few which do cover commercial use, for example, the exceptions for news reporting (s30(2)), apart from photographs, and criticism and review (s30(1)).

For further information on 'commercial purpose' see Section 3.2.2 on p. 42 and Figure 3.1 on p. 43.

8.1.2   Library exceptions and definition of 'library'

The library exceptions include:

- libraries and educational establishments making works available through dedicated terminals (section 40B of CDPA 1988)
- copying by librarians: supply of single copies to other libraries (section 41)

- copying by librarians: replacement copies of works (section 42)
- copying by librarians: single copies of published works (section 42A)
- copying by librarians or archivists: single copies of unpublished works (section 43).

The library exceptions were almost completely re-written in 2014, and they can be found in sections 40A–43A of the CDPA 1988. Corporate library and information professionals are not able to make use of these exceptions because the definition of a 'library' for the purposes of sections 40A–43 requires that the library be publicly accessible or a library of an educational establishment (the exceptions also cover museums and galleries), and that it be not for profit. The phrase 'conducted for profit', in relation to a library, archive or museum, means a body of that kind which is established or conducted for profit or which forms part of, or is administered by, a body established or conducted for profit.

8.2 Licensing

The copyright exceptions are by their nature limited in scope, and that is especially true for the corporate sector, where a significant portion of its copying would fall under the heading of copying for a commercial purpose. There are, however, a number of agencies that act on behalf of rights owners and issue licences that permit copying which would not otherwise be allowed. Licences are therefore an important way in which corporate library and information services are able to make use of content lawfully. Licensees are in effect paying for the privilege of being able to do more than the copyright exceptions would have allowed. The licence will set out what content it covers; who is permitted to use the content; and what uses they are allowed to make of that content.

One aspect of licensing is the types of licence available from the collective licensing societies. These act on behalf of a group of rights holders, for a specific category or type of material. For example, the Copyright Licensing Agency licences cover the use of books and journals and NLA Media Access licences cover the use of newspapers and some magazines.

8.2.1 Copyright Licensing Agency

The Copyright Licensing Agency has a number of licences for the corporate sector. These include:

- standard CLA business licence
- multinational business licence
- pharmaceutical and medcomms companies licence
- law firms licence.

The CLA's standard business licence does permit the storage of digital content in a central repository, but it is important to bear in mind that this is only permitted for a maximum of 30 days under the business licence.

8.2.2   NLA Media Access

NLA has a number of licences relevant to the corporate sector. These include:

- business licence
- corporate website republishing licence (which allows posting positive press coverage on your corporate website and social media).

8.2.3   Orphan works licensing

An orphan works licence (see Chapter 6) can be obtained either for commercial or for non-commercial use. 'Commercial use' would cover any uses that make money from the work – such as selling copies of the work or directly charging for access to it, regardless of whether those charges are intended to make a profit or are simply to cover costs. It would cover merchandizing or selling copies of a publication, and it would also cover commercial advertising, marketing or promotion activities.

There are two fees for taking out an orphan works licence, one being an administration fee and the other being a fee for the licence itself. The licence fee for non-commercial uses is nominal (10 pence per item), whereas the fee for commercial uses will be much higher. Licence fees are set by looking at the prices charged for using similar non-orphan works in the same way. In most instances, anyone wishing to apply for an orphan works licence will be able to see what the licence fee will be before completing their licence application. To find out how much the licence fee will be, simply select the work type you wish to use (such as a photograph) and the use or uses (such as use in a book), and the system will calculate the price. However, there are a small number of instances where the licence fee isn't shown but will instead be set on a 'price on application' basis, where the licence applicant is asked to e-mail the IPO, which will then quote a licence fee for that type of work and use.

8.2.4   Aggregator products

Another option would be to review the various aggregator services that are available, check whether they have the key publications that you use, and to see what activities are permitted under the licence agreement. That could help to avoid the need to negotiate individual agreements with many information providers; it could help to contain the costs; and it could help to ensure compliant usage of the content, because the licence agreements for information products can differ widely in terms of what they will and won't allow. Using an aggregator product will mean that a vast repertoire of content could be available under a single set of licence terms.

8.3   Image searching

If you intend to use images for a commercial purpose, it is worth making full use of the advanced search features available on the search engines. For example, if you use Google's advanced image search (www.google.com/advanced_image_search), scroll down to the heading for 'usage rights' and filter the search so that it is limited to searching for either records which are free to use or share even commercially, or which are free to use, share or modify even commercially. Similarly, with the image search facility on Bing (www.bing.com/images), do a search and then when the results appear use the drop-down for 'license' in order to select ones which are either free to share and use commercially or free to modify, share and use commercially.

8.4   Other means of getting permission to copy content

There are also services such as the Publishers Licensing Society service PLSclear, www.plsclear.com/Pages/ClearWizard.aspx

Further reading

International Chamber of Commerce (2007) *Model Intellectual Property Guidelines for Business: overview and guidance*, http://bascap.net/Guidelines/files/ BASCAP%20-%20Model%20IP%20 Guidelines%20-%20Guidance%20-% 20draft%203.2%20-%2017%20Oct%2007.pdf.

References and further reading

CILIP (2014) *Model Copyright Declaration Forms*,
www.cilip.org.uk/sites/default/files/documents/Declaration%20forms%20No
v%202014.pdf.

Depreeuw, Sari and Hubin, Jean-Benoit (2014) *Study on the Making Available
Right and its Relationship with the Reproduction Right in Cross-Border Digital
Transmissions*, De Wolf & Partners. European Union,
ISBN 978-92-79-33045-2.

Gowers, Andrew (2006) *Gowers Review of Intellectual Property*, HM Treasury,
www.gov.uk/government/publications/gowers-review-of-intellectual-property.

Hargreaves, Ian (2011) *Digital Opportunity: a review of intellectual property and growth*,
www.gov.uk/government/publications/digital-opportunity-review-of-
intellectual-property-and-growth.

Intellectual Property Office (2014) *Exceptions to Copyright: education and teaching*,
https://www.gov.uk/government/uploads/system/uploads/attachment_data/file
/375951/Education_and_Teaching.pdf.

Intellectual Property Office (2014) *Exceptions to Copyright: research*.

Intellectual Property Office (2014–) *IP for Business: events, guidance, tools and case
studies*, www.gov.uk/government/collections/ip-for-business-events-guidance-
tools-and-case-studies.

Intellectual Property Office (2014) *Licensing Intellectual Property*,
https://www.gov.uk/licensing-intellectual-property.

Intellectual Property Office (2015) *Non-disclosure Agreements*,
https://www.gov.uk/government/publications/non-disclosure-
agreements/non-disclosure-agreements.

Intellectual Property Office (2013) *Resolving IP Disputes*, IP Health Check 5,
https://www.gov.uk/government/uploads/system/uploads/attachment_data/
file/355845/Resolving_IP_Disputes.pdf.

Intellectual Property Office (2014) *Valuing Your Intellectual Property*,
https://www.gov.uk/valuing-your-intellectual-property.

International Association of Scientific, Technical and Medical Publishers (2008)

Guidelines for Quotation and Other Academic Uses of Excerpts from Journal Articles, http://ocw.kyoto-u.ac.jp/en/copyright-en/files/11Elsevier.pdf.

London Manifesto, www.cilip.org.uk/cilip/advocacy-campaigns-awards/advocacy-campaigns/copyright/london-manifesto.

Weatherley, Mike (2014) *Copyright Education and Awareness: a discussion paper,* www.mikeweatherleymp.com/wp-content/uploads/2014/10/11.pdf.

Index